And Slowly Beauty

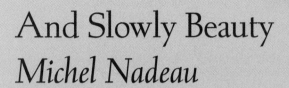

And Slowly Beauty
Michel Nadeau

with

Marie-Josée Bastien, Lorraine Côté,
Hugues Frenette, Pierre-François
Legendre, Véronika Makdissi-Warren,
and Jack Robitaille

Théâtre Niveau Parking

Translated by Maureen Labonté

Talonbooks

Talonbooks
P.O. Box 2076, Vancouver, British Columbia, Canada V6B 3S3
www.talonbooks.com

Typeset in Frutiger
Printed and bound in Canada on 100% post-consumer recycled paper
Cover design by Page & Design
Typeset by Typesmith

First printing: 2013

Talonbooks gratefully acknowledges the financial support of the Canada Council
for the Arts, the Government of Canada through the Canada Book Fund, and the
Province of British Columbia through the British Columbia Arts Council and
the Book Publishing Tax Credit.

Lentement la beauté by Michel Nadeau was first published in French by L'instant
même, Quebec City, Quebec, in 2004. We acknowledge the financial support of
the Government of Canada through the National Translation Program for Book
Publishing, for our publishing activities.

Rights to produce *And Slowly Beauty*, in whole or in part, in any medium by any
group, amateur or professional, are retained by the author. Interested persons are
requested to contact the author's agent: Catherine Mensour, l'Agence Mensour Agency,
41 chemin Springfield Road, Ottawa, Ontario K1M 1C8; telephone 613-241-1677;
fax 613-241-4360; email kate@mensour.ca.

LIBRARY AND ARCHIVES CANADA CATALOGUING IN PUBLICATION

Nadeau, Michel
[Lentement la beauté. English]
    And slowly beauty / Michel Nadeau ; with Marie-Josée Bastien,
Lorraine Côté, Hugues Frenette, Pierre-François Legendre, Véronika
Makdissi-Warren and Jack Robitaille ; translated by Maureen Labonté.

Originally published under title: Lentement la beauté.
Issued in print and electronic formats.
ISBN 978-0-88922-786-6 (pbk.). — ISBN 978-0-88922-787-3 (epub)

    I. Labonté, Maureen, 1949–, translator II. Title. III. Title: Lentement la beauté.
English

PS8639.H42L4613 2013   C842'.6   C2013-903576-1
                                                   C2013-903577-X

To Anton Chekhov, with immense gratitude

BEGINNINGS

For a number of years now, at Théâtre Niveau Parking, one of our main challenges when creating a new work is how to tap into and release the "genii" in the creative team. Yes, "genii." Like Aladdin and his lamp. It was our chief preoccupation as we started work on the original French version of *And Slowly Beauty* and it was our guiding spirit as we developed the play.

All we had, to start with, was an idea: a man goes to see a production of Chekhov's *Three Sisters* and leaves the theatre deeply moved and shaken.

I brought the creative team together and asked them these questions: Who is this man? What does he do? Why does the play move and disturb him? And how will it change him? We got into long discussions about the man himself, *Three Sisters*, Chekhov, and life.

Then, we started to improvise. We wanted to explore and deepen what we already knew about Mr. Mann. At the end of this first phase of the work, we had a much better idea about who he was and what his story might be.

Because Anton Chekhov was not just a playwright but also a well-known and accomplished short-story writer, I suggested that we write a short story together about Mr. Mann. One after the other, each of us wrote a few pages and, in relay fashion, passed them on to another member of the ensemble. We ended up with a forty-page short story that was the product of our collective imaginations but without some of the constraints and limitations of improvisation.

After this, we worked out a second outline for the play. Mr. Mann's story was becoming clearer and more detailed. We began another series of improvisations in order to develop the material even further, this time adding details of time, space, and place.

I gathered all these different elements together (outlines, improvisations, short story) and they became the raw material with which I wrote the play. As a result, *And Slowly Beauty* is a play written by a single writer but it was fed and made richer by months of work by the acting ensemble. So it's both my play and our play. That's what makes this way of working so alive, so vibrant, and so special.

– MICHEL NADEAU

And Slowly Beauty was first produced in French under the title *Lentement la beauté* by Théâtre Niveau Parking, April 1 to 26, 2003, at the Théâtre Périscope in Quebec City. The production toured extensively and was performed more than a hundred times on stages all over Quebec and throughout French Canada.

CAST

Jack Robitaille	Mr. Mann
Marie-Josée Bastien	Anita, Woman 2, Nurse, Olga, Mother
Lorraine Côté	Claudette, Nicole, Woman 1, Director, Girl 1, Friend 2, Wife, Masha, Young Woman 2
Hugues Frenette	Quentin, Man 1, Man 4, Vershinin, Bookstore Clerk, Male Nurse, Reporter, Friend 4, Jeff, Father, Boy 2, Tuzenbach
Pierre-François Legendre	Momo, Sylvain, Man 2, Man 3, Carrier, Young Man, Boy 1, Friend 1, Andrey, Husband, Chebutykin, Actor, Boyfriend
Véronika Makdissi-Warren	Nadine, Cathya, Woman 3, Woman 4, Irina, Girl 2, Young Woman 1, Actress
Director	Michel Nadeau
Assistant to the Director	Anne-Marie Olivier
Sets	Monique Dion
Costume Designer	Marie-Chantale Vaillancourt
Lighting Designer	Denis Guérette
Sound Designer	Yves Dubois

And Slowly Beauty, an English translation by Maureen Labonté, was read at the Canadian Stage Company in Toronto on May 16, 2010, as part of the 2010 Festival of Ideas and Creation. The reading was a collaboration between the Canadian Stage Company and the National Arts Centre (NAC) in Ottawa.

CAST

Michael Simpson	Mr. Mann
Diane D'Aquila	Anita, Woman 2, Nurse, Olga, Mother
Sarah Mennell	Claudette, Nicole, Woman 1, Director, Girl 1, Friend 2, Wife, Masha, Young Woman 2
Kevin Bundy	Quentin, Man 1, Man 4, Vershinin, Bookstore Clerk, Male Nurse, Reporter, Friend 4, Jeff, Father, Boy 2, Tuzenbach
Simon Rainville	Momo, Sylvain, Man 2, Man 3, Carrier, Young Man, Boy 1, Friend 1, Andrey, Husband, Chebutykin, Actor, Boyfriend
Natasha Greenblatt	Nadine, Cathya, Woman 3, Woman 4, Irina, Girl 2, Young Woman 1, Actress
Director	Peter Hinton
Dramaturg	Paula Danckert
Festival Coordinator	Natasha Mytnowytch

A NAC English Theatre / Belfry Theatre co-production of *And Slowly Beauty* was performed September 20 to October 23, 2011, at the Belfry Theatre in Victoria and from November 7 to 19, 2011, at the National Arts Centre in Ottawa.

CAST

Dennis Fitzgerald	Mr. Mann
Mary-Colin Chisholm	Anita, Woman 2, Nurse, Olga, Mother
Caroline Gillis	Claudette, Nicole, Woman 1, Director, Girl 1, Friend 2, Wife, Masha, Young Woman 2
Thomas Olajide	Quentin, Man 1, Man 4, Vershinin, Bookstore Clerk, Male Nurse, Reporter, Friend 4, Jeff, Father, Boy 2, Tuzenbach
Christian Murray	Momo, Sylvain, Man 2, Man 3, Carrier, Young Man, Boy 1, Friend 1, Andrey, Husband, Chebutykin, Actor, Boyfriend
Celine Stubel	Nadine, Cathya, Woman 3, Woman 4, Irina, Girl 2, Young Woman 1, Actress
Director	Michael Shamata
Designer	John Ferguson
Lighting Designer	Michael Walton
Sound Designer	Brooke Maxwell
Associate Designer	Tamara Marie Kucheran
Stage Manager	Kim Charleen Smith (Victoria) / Jane Vanstone Osborn (Ottawa)

CHARACTERS

MR. MANN, middle-aged, works in a large government agency

CLAUDETTE, his wife

NADINE, their daughter

QUENTIN, their son

NICOLE, a woman who sells newspapers on the street

MOMO, a young man with a mental handicap, Nicole's friend

ANITA, a woman who works at a café

SYLVAIN, Mr. Mann's younger friend and co-worker

CARRIER, another younger co-worker

CATHYA, a young woman artist

JEFF, an actor

A number of other characters, including JOGGER, PARK
EMPLOYEE, JANITOR, MALE NURSE, NURSE, BOOKSTORE
CLERK, REPORTER, ACTOR, ACTRESS, DIRECTOR, HUSBAND,
WIFE, MOTHER, FATHER, BOYFRIEND, BOYS, GIRLS, YOUNG
MAN, YOUNG WOMAN 1, YOUNG WOMAN 2, WOMAN, and
MEN, and characters from Chekhov's *Three Sisters*, including
IRINA, VERSHININ, TUZENBACH, and MASHA

SETTING

PLACE: Quebec City

TIME: The present

The action of the play takes place over a period of about a month.

A FEW NOTES ABOUT THE PRODUCTION

As I was preparing to direct *Lentement la beauté* for the first time,
I set out a few rules for myself – my rules of the game. Rule one:
keep it simple. I decided to do the play with only six chairs and
three small square-topped tables. By their very presence, these
prop-like set pieces imposed a rhythm on the *mise-en-scène*. We
sometimes had to change the order of the lines or even of the scene
sequences so that the movement or choreography of the tables and
chairs would be as seamless and organic as possible. In some ways,
the spatial language became as important as the words themselves.

Rule two had to do with the protagonist, Mr. Mann, and the
play's chorus. In this play, as in Greek tragedy, there is Mr. Mann
and then there are all the other characters who make up what could
be called "the chorus of his life." Some of these characters – like the
members of his family, or Anita, or his friend Sylvain – have a much
stronger, much more important presence or existence; however,
others merely pass through, fleetingly, as in life.

Another rule that was important for me in the staging of the
play is that the audience should always feel this movement –
the flow and rhythm Mr. Mann is caught up in. An image kept
coming back to me, that of a stone with a coursing river flowing
over and around it. Fish swimming to and fro, coming and going,
darting and circling. That's why the actors play many characters
with minimal costume changes or scene changes. I wanted the
audience to always feel this continual flow or movement rather
than present them with a series of connected, but separate, scenes.
That's also why the lines from *Three Sisters* quoted in the play are
more important than the characters who are saying them and why
the same actor can speak the lines of more than one of Chekhov's
characters in the same scene.

And the last rule was that, contrary to the dictates of traditional
theatre, there would be no conflict played out openly onstage. Both
the writing and the staging of the play should allow the audience
to experience the drama within themselves rather than see it acted
out or "ignited" onstage.

– MICHEL NADEAU

And Slowly Beauty

*The ACTOR playing Mr. Mann enters and speaks to
the audience.*

ACTOR

A man gets ready to go to work. This happens every day.

MORNING

MR. MANN stands in front of his mirror at home.

*He has a big meeting at the office today. He has to oversee
the implementation of a new government reform, and his
first major task since a recent, but temporary, promotion
to take over from a colleague on sick leave, is to present a
restructuring plan.*

*He looks at his face. He feels old. He finishes dressing: the top
button of his shirt, his tie, his jacket. He looks at himself again:
he's ready. He exits.*

THE STREET

*On the street, there are lots of people all walking quickly.
MR. MANN's pace is different from the rest.*

*Through the window of a café, we see a waitress, ANITA,
having a lively and pleasant conversation with a customer
who can't be seen.*

*Suddenly, MR. MANN notices NICOLE, a young woman
squatting against a wall selling copies of* Outreach, *a
newspaper for and by the homeless.*

NICOLE

Outreach. Outreach. Newspaper for the homeless. *Outreach.*

*No one stops. We hear a flock of geese flying overhead,
but no one seems to hear them. MR. MANN decides to buy
a copy of the newspaper. When the sale is completed, NICOLE
leaves. He watches her go. Then he continues to walk to work,
reading the front page of the paper as he enters the office.*

There's as much movement and rushing around in the office as there was on the street, but now the silhouettes are more individualized. We see the surge of activity that precedes the beginning of a workday.

MR. MANN stops at the water cooler. After drinking a glass of water, he reviews his notes for the meeting. WOMAN 1 and WOMAN 2 enter.

WOMAN 1
I was so shocked when I saw him lying there! Tubes sticking out of him! Last week, he was so full of life!

WOMAN 2
And, we don't know anything, we don't know whether it's serious or not.

WOMAN 1
Of course it's serious.

WOMAN 2
And Joanne, what do you think she's going to do?

WOMAN 1
I don't know.

WOMAN 2
Three children. When there are children involved, I ...

MR. MANN
Who? Who's in the hospital?

WOMAN 1 and WOMAN 2
Mark!

MR. MANN
Mark ...

WOMAN 1
Mark in *Straight to the Heart*. The TV show.

MR. MANN
Aah!

WOMAN 1
You don't watch it?

MR. MANN
No.

WOMAN 1 and WOMAN 2
You don't watch *Straight to the Heart*!

MR. MANN
I don't watch much television.

WOMAN 2
Oh, you should. Even people who usually don't like TV like *Straight to the Heart*.

WOMAN 1
It's bound to win a Gemini. (*as she's leaving*) Did you get a look at Rachel's face?

WOMAN 2
Oh, I hate her!

> *They leave. MAN 1 and WOMAN 3 enter and cross the stage talking.*

WOMAN 3
They cut our budget. They want us to do more, but they cut the budget!

MAN 1
Don't talk to me about it. The problem's upstairs.

WOMAN 3
They cut the budget!

MAN 1
Do more with less! Personally, I do less with less!

WOMAN 3
They cut the budget but we still have to perform.

MAN 1
At this rate, I'm heading straight for a three-month sick leave. Like Monique!

> *They exit. MAN 2 enters and comes over to MR. MANN.*

MAN 2

Hey! How you doing?

MR. MANN

Hi.

MAN 2

I'm organizing the Christmas party this year and we have a choice between two clowns or karaoke. Which do you prefer?

MR. MANN

The Christmas party! But it isn't even summer yet!

MAN 2

No, but if we want to get what we want, this is the perfect time. So, clowns or karaoke?

MR. MANN

...

MAN 2

Karaoke, okay?

MR. MANN

Okay.

MAN 2

Okay! Perfect. (*to himself as he exits*) No goddamn clowns this year.

WOMAN 4 enters. She's in a hurry. She sees MR. MANN and makes a beeline for him.

WOMAN 4

Hello! Have you put your name down for the raffle?

MR. MANN

What raffle?

WOMAN 4

The social committee's. You could win a pair of tickets to the theatre. Can I put you down?

MR. MANN

Okay. Tickets for what?

WOMAN 4

(*as she's leaving in as much of a hurry as before*) I don't know. Helen was supposed to be looking after this. I've got so much work and everyone keeps dumping stuff on my desk 'cause they're swamped. And I'm not, I suppose!

> *MAN 3 and MAN 4 also approach the water cooler.*

MAN 3

It's an ethical question. It's simple really. It's all a matter of ethics.

MAN 4

Josée di Stasio[1] says that –

MAN 3

Josée di Stasio. Pinard put her on the map. I'm a Pinard man all the way and if Pinard – (*notices MR. MANN*) Hi.

MR. MANN

Hi.

MAN 3

Hey, here's one for you. Let's suppose you're making Pinard's tomato pie and you run out of ricotta, what would you use? This guy here says mascarpone.

MAN 4

You could.

MAN 3

Mascarpone is a dessert cheese.

MAN 4

Not necessarily.

MAN 3

I say you use feta and cut out the salt.

MR. MANN

Yeah ... goat cheese maybe? If it's not too strong ...

---

1   Josée di Stasio and Daniel Pinard are well-known celebrity chefs in Quebec.

MAN 3

No, no, no! Goat cheese! No.

MAN 4

Yeah but feta –

MAN 3

Goat cheese changes everything!

MAN 4

But you're suggesting feta and it's made from sheep's milk.

MAN 3

Yes, but ... look ... Montreal is closer to Quebec City than Ottawa, right?
With goat cheese, you're in Ottawa.

MAN 4

Ah, but if you use mascarpone, my friend, you're just a ferry ride across
the river in Lévis.

MAN 3

You've got to be kidding! Do you believe this guy?! (*to MR. MANN*)
Are you okay? You usually go along with our –

MR. MANN

Oh ... it's just that ... I've got a big meeting in a little while. With the gang
from downstairs. I'm presenting the new restructuring plan.

MAN 3

Monique's people?

MAN 4

That's right! You're replacing her.

MR. MANN

Yeah.

MAN 3 and MAN 4

(*joking*) Oh boy! I wouldn't want to be in your shoes.

MAN 4

So do you understand it ... the new restructuring plan?!

> *MAN 3 and MAN 4 laugh.*

MR. MANN

I have to.

MAN 3

Right! The skill set comes with the promotion!

MAN 4

And what a promotion!

MR. MANN

We're here to serve.

MAN 3 and MAN 4

(*as they leave*) Okay then ... see you! Good luck!

    WOMAN 1 and WOMAN 2 come back to the water cooler.

WOMAN 1

I'm telling you, I was stunned when I found out! He's always got so much energy.

WOMAN 2

And we don't know anything. We don't know if it's serious.

WOMAN 1

No. Let's hope it's not.

WOMAN 2

And Madeleine. Did she say anything else?

WOMAN 1

No.

WOMAN 2

Two children. If anything happens ... when there are children involved ...

MR. MANN

Mark isn't any better?

WOMAN 1

Mark? Who's Mar–? No, no, we're talking about Sylvain!

WOMAN 2

Sylvain's in the hospital.

MR. MANN

Sylvain? Our Sylvain!

WOMAN 1 and WOMAN 2
Yes.

MR. MANN
When?

WOMAN 1
Yesterday. He took a day off work because he wasn't feeling well. He went to see the doctor and the doctor decided to admit him and run a whole series of tests.

WOMAN 2
It could be he's just exhausted. Accumulated fatigue, you know. Sometimes our bodies have a way of sending us an alarm signal. The body's a whole lot smarter than we are.

MR. MANN
What hospital?

WOMAN 1
Saint-Sacrament. There's a card on the bulletin board if you want to sign it. We're sending it to him tomorrow.

MR. MANN
Yes, sure, of course. Thank you.

WOMAN 1 and WOMAN 2
You're welcome.

WOMAN 1
(*as she's leaving*) I wonder if Marielle is going to sign it. The face on that one!

WOMAN 2
Oh, I can't stand her!

>   *Three women rush by, including WOMAN 4. She stops*
>   *suddenly and speaks to MR. MANN.*

WOMAN 4
Did you sign up for the ...? Oh yes. You did.

>   *And she rushes out. MR. MANN looks at his watch and heads*
>   *for the meeting room.*

> *MR. MANN is anxious. He checks his notes. He paces up and down. He doesn't feel ready. He looks at his watch.*

MR. MANN

What's going on? I hope I've got the right room.

> *Suddenly, he hears people arriving. To him, they sound like a thundering horde. Actors armed with chairs descend upon him. They all take a seat and throughout this scene respond, first in unison as a CHORUS, and then individually as indistinct voices.*

MR. MANN

First of all, I'd like to thank you for being here and for being so punctual. Since we don't have a lot of time, I'll try to be clear and to the point. So. You all received a copy of the agenda for today's meeting.

CHORUS

Mm-hmm.

MR. MANN

I also sent you a few support documents: the guide and the minutes of the last two meetings with Monique.

CHORUS

Mm-hmm.

MR. MANN

As you can see, the agenda is fairly straightforward; only one item: a review of the new restructuring plan.

CHORUS

Mm-hmm.

MR. MANN

I suppose you could call it the restructuring of the restructuring plan! (*silence*) So, in order to bring us up to speed on the latest developments with regards to that, and because of events which you are all aware of, management has decided to suspend the entire review process which had already been set in motion and to extend the restructuring to include all vertical management procedures, from top to bottom, as well as all the lateral ramifications impacting other divisions of this institution.

CHORUS
    Mm-hmm.

MR. MANN
    Now, rather than only visioning the restructuring vertically, the way it
    was intended at the outset ...

CHORUS
    Mm-hmm.

MR. MANN
    In silos.

CHORUS
    Mm-hmm.

MR. MANN
    We are going to re-vision it vertically *and* horizontally.

CHORUS
    Mm-hmm.

MR. MANN
    As I'm sure you're aware, the mandate is a huge one.

CHORUS
    Mm-hmm.

MR. MANN
    Much broader in scope than initially laid out. However, the deadlines
    remain the same.

        Silence.

    That's the way it is. We don't have a choice in the matter. It's an
    enormous task, I know.

        Silence.

    Of course no one has time for this. We all have piles of work on our
    desks. But we still have to do it. And (*shrugging*) somehow we always
    manage to get the job done.

        Silence.

    That's why I decided to get the ball rolling by setting up a smaller
    committee like this one. And since each one of your jobs shares
    convergence points with other divisional nerve centres, it's important to

have your input on everything that touches the lateral and transversal aspects of the restructuring. This committee will be a kind of super subcommittee, if you like.

> *The mood shifts. Now the actors respond as indistinct voices. The actual lines spoken by the various voices should be barely comprehensible, with the dialogue in square brackets showing the intended meaning of each line; all the audience hears is the music of the lines as delivered by each of the actors in the tone of voice suggested. The dialogue begins with the kind of office worker who's always muttering comments to the person sitting next to him.*

SOTTO VOCE VOICE
... [*We* don't!]

> *Everyone laughs.*

MR. MANN
We don't! Aah! That's a good one, a good one! No ... but joking aside, this is important because afterwards you're the ones who are going to have to sell the whole thing to your people, to your troops.

SELF-PITYING VOICE
... [But does that mean we now have to start all over?]

MR. MANN
No, no! Not at all! Thank you for raising that point, Melanie. All the work you've done so far won't be wasted. We should be able to salvage a substantial part of it. It'll simply be a matter of orienting it a bit differently. And, expanding it a little, right? Expanding it.

NASAL VOICE
... [So now, the major axes and all that are gone?]

MR. MANN
No, no, no! On the contrary! We keep the six major axes. I don't know how well you remember the main points of the plan. The six major axes, each with its own individual set of objectives and main evaluation criteria have now been added to the two other major sections, or super sections I suppose we could call them, which in turn correspond directly to the three main themes described on the first page of the document.

NASAL VOICE

... [Like transparency?]

MR. MANN

No, that's not a section, that's an axis. Number 3, I believe ... uh ...
I'm not entirely sure. That's a very good point. I'll have to check and
get back to you on that.

HIGH-PITCHED VOICE

... ... (*many words delivered very fast*) [These reforms will have a huge
impact on the day-to-day organization of our work.]

MR. MANN

Yes.

HIGH-PITCHED VOICE

... ...

MR. MANN

Yes.

HIGH-PITCHED VOICE

... ...

MR. MANN

Yes.

HIGH-PITCHED VOICE

... ...

MR. MANN

Of ...?

HIGH-PITCHED VOICE

... (*very brief*)

MR. MANN

Oh! Okay.

HIGH-PITCHED VOICE

... (*continuing to protest*)

MR. MANN

Listen, I think we're going to have to stick to the agenda, because if we open that up for discussion, we'll be here all week.

NASAL VOICE

... [Yes, but what she's saying is true.]

MR. MANN

Yes, yes, of course, and it is very relevant. However ... time is a major factor here as I'm sure you can appreciate. The timeline is very tight. (*to HIGH-PITCHED VOICE*) Look, I've made a note of it and perhaps we could add it to the agenda of another meeting as a special point for discussion. Is that okay?

HIGH-PITCHED VOICE

... [Okay.]

MR. MANN

Good. Do any of you have suggestions relating specifically to your sectors based on what you've read in the document?

Silence.

MR. MANN

Suggestions, comments.

A longer silence.

CRANKY VOICE

... [Maybe we could create links with the regional offices?]

MR. MANN

Yes! I totally agree! There's a link to be made with that whole sector, you're absolutely right. And that reminds me: everything related to our social programs, particularly for young people – sponsorships, scholarships, parks – have to be protected at all costs. Melanie, do you think you could prepare an overview of everything we do in those areas at a local, provincial, and national level?

SELF-PITYING VOICE

... [Well ... I'm swamped right now!]

MR. MANN

I know, I know, we all have a lot of work. But you're not alone, you
know, you can get help.

SELF-PITYING VOICE

... [Well, I can't actually. Brigitte and Josée have left.]

MR. MANN

They left! ... I didn't know that. Have they been replac–? Uh ...
listen, uh ...

NASAL VOICE

... [She can't do all that by herself. This reform doesn't make any sense.]

MR. MANN

Listen, everyone, change is never easy. Don't think – Look, we have to
be proactive in this process. It's not a matter of solving all the problems
today. But it makes sense to me to pool our resources in order to, to, to
encourage synergy in our actions, our efforts, that's all.

CRANKY VOICE

... [When is Monique coming back?]

MR. MANN

Monique? Not for three months. All right, listen, this is serious.
Management wants a plan of action in three months. All I ask is that
we put some ideas down on paper – ideas which are pertinent. Like
the document says: pertinent, effective, consistent, and contingent.

SOTTO VOCE VOICE

... [Confluent!]

MR. MANN

Confluent. Ah, good one! Very good.

HIGH-PITCHED VOICE

... ... (*She's not happy.*)

MR. MANN

Now, that's your point of view and I respect it.

NASAL VOICE

... ... (*She's not happy either.*)

SELF-PITYING VOICE

... ... (*Nor is she.*)

MR. MANN

No, but ... listen ...

ALL VOICES

... ... (*No one's happy.*)

> *MR. MANN tries to make himself heard. Everyone's talking at the same time. Suddenly, he grabs his copy of* Outreach.

MR. MANN

Please, everyone! Listen! Listen to me! (*waving the newspaper in the air*) Do any of you know this newspaper? When we go out to buy our sandwiches every day at lunch, there's always a young girl selling it on the corner. It's a paper for and by street kids. We're working for them as well. The restructuring is for them too. It's all well and good to merge and restructure, but we have a social mission and we shouldn't forget that. It was the rationale behind the setting up of this agency. Remember our one guiding principle: to be close to the people, to each and every individual in need, to the grassroots, and, particularly, to young people. Like these kids. Young people who, who, who are hungry, who have nothing in their stomachs, and who, if we aren't vigilant – How many of you know the song "The Impossible Dream"? From *Man of La Mancha*? That's what we're going to do! Without question or pause. We're going to fight until we get through this. I'm dead serious. It's going be a helluva rough ride, but if we hold on, we'll get through it! We've gotta hold on real tight! Do you hear me!

> *Silence.*

SOTTO VOCE VOICE

... (*about to make another joke*)

> *MR. MANN interrupts.*

MR. MANN

Please, this is not the time! (*silence*) All right. Is there anything anyone would like to add?

> *Silence.*

MR. MANN

We'll stop here for today if that's all right with you. Next meeting ... let's say ... next week, same time? Is that okay with everyone?

HIGH-PITCHED VOICE

...?

MR. MANN

Same room, yes. Thank you all. See you next week.

> *They leave. MR. MANN is not happy with the meeting or his performance. The job ahead is going to be onerous and he doesn't feel that he's the right person to see it through. He leaves the office.*

THE STREET

> *On his way back home, he sees the café and, on a whim, decides to go in. Everyone looks up at him as he enters. On second thought, he's not too sure that he feels like being with a crowd of people. He leaves.*

> *He runs to catch his bus. The bus is full. He has to stand. He reads the paper. MOMO, who is sitting on one of the bench seats, says hello to him, a greeting he returns, but shyly. MOMO points to the newspaper.*

MOMO

Outreach!

> *MR. MANN nods.*

MOMO

(*raising his thumb*) *Prends soin!*

> *MR. MANN gets off the bus and heads home.*

AT HOME

> *MR. MANN enters the house.*

MR. MANN

It's me! (*silence*) Claudette! (*silence*)

> *Exhausted, he puts down his briefcase as though it has the weight of the world inside it. And then ...*

Claudette!

> *He notices a Post-it note on the back of the sofa.*

"I've gone to show a house. Will be back at four thirty. Claudette."

He looks at his watch. It's nearly six o'clock. He sees another Post-it.

"I had to go out again. Don't wait. Have supper without me. There's chicken in a Tupperware dish in the fridge. Kiss. Kiss."

He finds yet another Post-it.

"I read Mom's message. I'm going to study at Hugo's place. I'll be back in the morning. Nadine."

MR. MANN goes into the kitchen. Looks around the empty house. Finds another Post-it.

"Your mother phoned. You really should give her a call. Claudette."

He opens the fridge door and takes out the Tupperware dish. A Post-it stuck to the lid.

"Sorry. I ate it. Quentin."

He puts the Tupperware dish back in the fridge. Asks himself what he's going to do. Finally, he grabs a Post-it and a pencil.

(*writing*) "I won two tickets to the theatre. Have gone to eat supper in town."

While MR. MANN is writing, QUENTIN enters writing a Post-it too.

MR. MANN
   Ah! You're home.

QUENTIN
   Hi, Dad.

MR. MANN
   Didn't you hear me?

QUENTIN
   Well no, I was in my room with my headphones on. What're you doing?

MR. MANN
   I'm writing a note to your mother to tell her I'm going to the theatre tonight.

QUENTIN

The theatre?

MR. MANN

Yes. I won two tickets at the office and I thought I'd go with your mother, but now ...

QUENTIN

Do you have to?

MR. MANN

No, but at thirty dollars a ticket I'm definitely going. I never win anything.

QUENTIN

Oh, okay. I was writing her a note too. Could you give it to her?

MR. MANN

Sure.

QUENTIN hands him the note.

MR. MANN

Oh no, wait, I can't. I'll be gone before she gets back. (*thinks*) What am I saying? Give it to me. I'll stick it on with mine.

QUENTIN

Here.

MR. MANN

Thanks. Hey! Don't suppose you'd like to come with me?

QUENTIN

No. Thanks though. I'm going over to Latch's.[2]

MR. MANN

You can go over to Latch's some other night. You're always over there.

QUENTIN

What's the show?

MR. MANN

A group of young actors are putting it on. In a big loft on Christophe-Colomb. Apparently, it's very good. Modern. The play's a classic, but the production's modern. The reviews have been very good.

---

2   Quentin's best friend's family name is Lachance; hence his nickname, Latch.

QUENTIN

It's 'cause I told Latch I'd be there tonight and ...

MR. MANN

Okay, fine.

QUENTIN

Hey, Dad, you owe me forty bucks.

MR. MANN

I do?

QUENTIN

I finished painting the balcony this afternoon. I only have the trim around the roof and the birdhouses left.

MR. MANN gives him the money.

QUENTIN

Thanks. I checked out the trellis under the veranda and it could use doing too. That'd be a week's work. I could do it for a hundred bucks.

MR. MANN

Okay.

QUENTIN

Perfect. Okay, so, see ya. Have a good evening anyway.

MR. MANN

See ya.

QUENTIN leaves. MR. MANN is alone with the Post-it. He finishes writing his note.

MR. MANN

(*writing*) "I should be back around eleven." (*He thinks about this and changes it.*) "Eleven thirty." (*thinks about it again and ...*) "Eleven fifteen. See you later. Kiss. Kiss. Kiss."

He sticks the two Post-its one beside the other and takes one of the theatre tickets out of his pocket.

Three Sisters. By Anton Chekhov.

Three women enter followed by two men. With their entrances, we're in the theatre.

MR. MANN looks for a seat. It's the first time he's ever been to this kind of performance space. He looks all around. He looks at the other members of the audience, one by one.

There's a well-dressed WOMAN, sitting very straight, legs crossed, reading the program. A YOUNG MAN and a YOUNG WOMAN are in conversation. A MAN who looks tired gets up to let someone pass. Then another WOMAN also stands. Humming to herself, she takes off her coat and places it carefully on the back of her seat so that she'll be more comfortable.

The house lights dim. The audience settles. The YOUNG MAN kisses the YOUNG WOMAN. We hear the preshow music. Everyone is very attentive, preparing to watch what happens onstage; then, one by one, the members of the audience get up and disappear into the wings. In the end, only MR. MANN is left alone in the audience watching the play.

Each group of lines represents different scenes from Chekhov's Three Sisters, *and the actors say the lines of a number of different characters.*

– "It's Irina's birthday today!"

    Exclamations of joy.

– "Where are the cakes?"

– "What a marvellous day."

– "Wait! There are thirteen of us at the table!"

– "What? Don't tell me you've become superstitious."

– "I often say to myself, what if one could erase one's life and start again, but consciously this time. Let's suppose that the life we've already lived was simply a trial run, a first draft so to speak, and the other one, the real one. Then, I'd imagine, each and every one of us would make a concerted effort not to repeat ourselves."

– "The mummers are coming tonight."

– "Oh yes! The mummers!"

– "Let's drink cognac and play the piano all night long."

– "Where is my past? Where has it disappeared to? Once, I was young, carefree, intelligent; I had beautiful dreams and wonderful ideas; my present and my future were bright and full of hope ..."

– "I'll have to look for another job. Mine lacks poetry."
– "When I'm alone, everything is fine; however, when I'm with others, in society, I say the silliest things."

– "It is possible that this life, which we accept without a word, will one day seem strange and stupid, perhaps even shameful."

– "Moscow! Moscow!"

– "My Lord, what a fire!"
– "It's horrible!"
– "The doctor wasn't able to save her."
– "What will become of her children?"
– "They'll sleep in our room."
– "I beg of you, let us leave. Let us leave for Moscow!"

– "And there you are, life is over."

– "Life doesn't change. It is immutable. Look at the birds migrating, the geese, for example. They fly, they fly. They fly without knowing either why or where they're going. And what does it matter, as long as they are flying."
– "But still, what is the meaning of it all?"
– "The meaning ... Look, it's snowing. What is the meaning of that?"

– "Moscow! Moscow! Moscow!"

> *The actors return to their places in the audience. The lights come up. The audience applauds. Carried away by the show, MR. MANN stands and shouts.*

MR. MANN
  Bravo!

> *Suddenly, one of the audience members turns and speaks.*

– "It's Irina's birthday today!"

> *All the audience members get up to prepare for Irina's party. While they're placing the chairs, yet again, we hear the lines from the top of the opening sequence up to: "Don't tell me you've become superstitious." Enthralled, MR. MANN listens. When the actors exit, he is back home.*

AT HOME

> *CLAUDETTE is very tired. Wearing a bathrobe and half-reclining on the living room sofa, she listens as her husband tells her about the show he's just seen.*

MR. MANN

It was extraordinary! It was like a big celebration, a party! We were transported somewhere else. I never thought theatre could be as good as that!

CLAUDETTE

What was it about?

MR. MANN

Oh my goodness ... it was ... uh ... it was about three sisters who grew up in Moscow. At some point, their father moves them to a small provincial town. When the play starts, he's been dead for a year and the three sisters want to move back to Moscow. And for the entire play – it takes place over a number of years – they desperately want to go back to Moscow but they never will.

CLAUDETTE

Sounds kind of boring.

MR. MANN

It might seem boring ... yes ... it might ... told like that, but ... it's just that, well, there really isn't much of a story but it was very, very good. Full of amazing insights, reflections about life. There were a few ... I swear there were moments when I'd've stopped the play if I could have and asked them to repeat what they just said. That's how ... how incredibly ...

CLAUDETTE

Oh.

MR. MANN

It's a drama. At least, I think it's a drama but, somehow, you've got a
smile on your face the whole time. I don't know ... it was very special.
It was as though ... the characters were all stuck but ... somehow it was
about ... freedom!

CLAUDETTE

You know, I didn't sell that house.

MR. MANN

Oh no.

CLAUDETTE

No. That bloody house. I knew I should never have accepted the
contract. She's asking too much and, with all the work that needs to
be done, no one's going to buy it.

MR. MANN

But I thought that young couple was really interested.

CLAUDETTE

Yeah but he got a promotion and they've decided to stay in Sherbrooke.
Well, that's what they told me, but I think she didn't want to move
because of the children. Anyway ... I'm not sure it was such a good idea
to start a career at forty-two.

MR. MANN

Oh stop it. You were agent of the month almost as soon as you started.

CLAUDETTE

Beginner's luck. You know what I think, I think they rig it like that so
you'll stay.

MR. MANN

You know very well that's not true.

*She's so tired she could easily fall asleep while they're talking.
Her voice is getting lower and lower.*

CLAUDETTE

You never know. I'm too old for this.

MR. MANN
You shouldn't stress about it. It's not the end of the world if you don't sell three houses a month.

CLAUDETTE
I know that ... but ... I've got my pride ... and if I'm going to be rotten at it ... I'd rather ... I'd rather stay home ... I didn't think that ...

She's muttering now. Whatever she's now saying is inaudible. She stops talking. A pause.

MR. MANN
Are you asleep?

CLAUDETTE
Whaaat? No. I'm resting my eyes.

She falls asleep leaning on him. He looks at her and then at the room. Silence and a big, everyday emptiness. Suddenly, a gentle moaning can be heard. Very soft and low. MR. MANN tries to figure out where it's coming from. Is it outside? Through the open window. Probably, a neighbour. A woman in the next building making love. MR. MANN listens. We can hear her more and more clearly. CLAUDETTE wakes up. MR. MANN laughs a little, ill at ease.

MR. MANN
Listen.

CLAUDETTE
What?

MR. MANN
Listen!

CLAUDETTE
(*sitting up and listening*) Those two are always at it. Well, good night.

She hands him the remote control.

MR. MANN
Good night.

She stands. Her sore hip makes her limp.

MR. MANN

    Why don't you heat up your Magic Bag.

> *He watches her leave. The neighbour can still be heard.*
> *He listens. MR. MANN decides to close the window.*
> *He starts to leave but stops.*

> *He's not sleepy. He looks around the room, checks his watch,*
> *goes and sits back down on the couch, turns on the TV and*
> *watches it for a few seconds. Turns it off. His mind is*
> *elsewhere. He lies down on the couch. He's thinking*
> *of the play.*

BREAKFAST

> *MR. MANN has slept on the couch all night. He begins to*
> *dress the way he did before. This time, however, he has*
> *trouble buttoning the top button of his shirt and knotting his*
> *tie just right. Once he's finished dressing, the family enters*
> *for breakfast. It's the usual rush. But this morning, he's not*
> *in sync with the rest of the family.*

> *The characters' lines overlap and run into each in a*
> *choreographed hubbub of conversation.*

CLAUDETTE

    Morning, everyone!

NADINE

    (*arriving home from Hugo's*) Mom, I've got my German exam
this morning.

CLAUDETTE

    I feel great this morning.

NADINE

    You going to be able to give me a lift?

CLAUDETTE

    I slept really well. When I woke up everything was crystal clear. This
morning I know exactly what I have to do.

QUENTIN

    (*taking a Pop-Tart*) Berry Delight?!

CLAUDETTE
I visualized it.

NADINE
Who bought white bread?

CLAUDETTE
I saw myself selling it.

QUENTIN
I hate Berry Delight.

NADINE
Who bought white bread?!

CLAUDETTE
I did. I got it at the corner store. I was in a hurry.

NADINE
I'll grab breakfast at the university. (*exiting to her bedroom*) I'm going to be late again, I just know it.

CLAUDETTE
As I fell asleep, I was signing the offer to purchase.

QUENTIN
(*on his cellphone*) Hey, Latch.

CLAUDETTE
I slept like a log! (*to her husband*) I didn't hear you come to bed and I didn't hear you get up. Here's your coffee.

QUENTIN
(*on his cell*) Yeah.

CLAUDETTE
Look at you, you're all crumpled. Did you stay up all night? I hate that tie.

QUENTIN
(*on his cell*) Yeah.

NADINE

(*coming back into the kitchen*) Mom! Can you give me a lift? I've got an exam this morning and before that I have to go to the registrar's office.

QUENTIN

(*on his cell*) Yeah.

CLAUDETTE

Yes, I said I'll drive you. I'm almost finished my coffee.

NADINE

Quentin, I saw Claude yesterday. You've gotta bring him your CV. Hi, Dad.

CLAUDETTE

(*writing a to-do list*) Oh right, I mustn't forget to call Mrs. Turcotte today. She's already called me twice. I'll go by the office and pick up the papers. That means I'll also have to call the notary.

QUENTIN

(*to Latch*) Okay, I'll go.

NADINE

Mom, we've got to leave right now. I'm going to be late!

CLAUDETTE

Yes, yes, I'm coming.

QUENTIN

(*on his cell*) 'kay, bye.

CLAUDETTE

Hey, everyone, the cleaning lady's coming this morning, did you pick up after yourselves?

NADINE and QUENTIN

Yes.

QUENTIN

Mom, can you drop me off at Latch's place?

CLAUDETTE

Yes, but we're leaving right now.

NADINE
(*as she's heading out the door*) Great! I'm going to be late again.

QUENTIN
See ya, Dad.

> *QUENTIN leaves along with CLAUDETTE. She comes back and gives her husband a kiss.*

CLAUDETTE
Have a good day, dear.

> *She leaves.*

> *Silence.*

> *He looks around his house. He takes a sip of coffee. It tastes awful.*

THE STREET

> *MR. MANN walks along the street. He's moving at a pace completely different from everyone else. They're all hurrying to get to work the same as every morning. He looks at all these people rushing here, running there. NICOLE, the young girl selling* Outreach, *is sitting in the same spot.*

NICOLE
Outreach. Outreach.

> *MR. MANN buys another copy of the paper. NICOLE thanks him and then leaves.*

AT THE OFFICE

> *CARRIER enters MR. MANN's office.*

CARRIER
Hey, how you doing?

MR. MANN
Hi.

CARRIER
Did you get my email about the pension fund?

MR. MANN

I got it but I haven't read it yet. Haven't had time.

CARRIER

Okay, it's just that there's an information session about it this afternoon and I'm the person in charge.

MR. MANN

Okay.

CARRIER

And now, with the latest round of negotiations, they've made us a very, very interesting offer. You've been here since uh ... it must be ...

MR. MANN

I started as soon as I finished school.

CARRIER

Okay. Full time since then?

MR. MANN

No, I was part time for a good ten years.

CARRIER

Right. I'm not disturbing you, am I?

MR. MANN

No, no.

CARRIER

Okay. You know that, before, you couldn't buy years of seniority. Cost an arm and a leg. But now, with this new offer, it'd hardly cost you anything! They're going to convert or credit your days of sick leave! I'll bet you haven't claimed that many sick days, right?

MR. MANN

Not a single one.

CARRIER

Well, that's perfect then. They'll credit them all and at fifty-five you'll be able to claim 70 percent of your salary! I had them figure it out for me, and with tax brackets and all that, 70 percent of my salary ... you know what the difference from my net salary would be?

MR. MANN

No, I don't.

CARRIER

Six thousand! Six thousand dollars and I'm sitting on my patio!

MR. MANN

That's good.

CARRIER

Good?! You're telling me it's good! My goal: Patio Fifty-Five! Peace
and quiet! Won't even read the newspaper! For me, right now, my
retirement plan is my life plan! You're ... what? Forty ...

MR. MANN

Forty-eight.

CARRIER

Forty-eight! ... You tough it out until fifty-five and then: thank you,
folks, and good night! You're sitting on that patio of yours for the rest
of your days. I've got a brother-in-law; at fifty-five, he up and sold
everything. Everything! Then he fixed up one of those Prevost tour
buses; you know, the big fancy ones.

MR. MANN

Yeah, yeah.

CARRIER

Fixed it up real nice. Washer, dryer, the works ...

*While MR. MANN's dynamic younger colleague keeps talking,
the Chekhov character VERSHININ walks across the stage.
MR. MANN watches him.*

VERSHININ

"You know, I often wonder what it would be like if you could start
your life over again – deliberately, I mean, consciously ... Suppose you
could put aside the life you've lived already, as though it was just a
kind of rough draft, and then start another one which would be the
final version. If that happened, I think the thing you'd want most of all
would be not to repeat yourself. At the very least you'd try to create a
new environment for yourself, a house like this one, for instance, with
flowers and plenty of light ... I have a wife, you know, and two little

girls; my wife's not very well and all ... Well, if I could start my life all over again, I wouldn't marry ... No, no. I wouldn't!"

VERSHININ exits.

CARRIER

... he met another woman, younger than him, next picture ... the Yukon!

MR. MANN

Can I ask you ... if you had the choice to start over, would you do the same again?

CARRIER

You bet I would. With what I know today?! Absolutely! I can't see myself buying seniority at the beginning of my career. I'd have only gotten myself into debt for nothing –

MR. MANN

No, no. I'm talking about starting over at square one.

CARRIER

What do you mean, at square – If you start over at square one, it doesn't work; you lose everything, you can't buy anything back.

MR. MANN

No, I'm talking about life! Doesn't it depress you to look at things that way? Don't you find it all a ... a load of crap?

CARRIER

What are you – I'm talking to you about your retirement plan. I'm not talking to you about life!

MR. MANN

Well, I am! Don't you find it deeply depressing to hear yourself talk that way? You just turned thirty and all you dream about is getting old. You're young and you're already dead!

CARRIER

Hey! Whoa! Slow down a minute. I just stopped by to invite you to a meeting. If you're having problems with your retirement, it doesn't give you the right to go after me like that. No projecting, please! Male menopause can be treated, ya know! As an employee, there's a support program you can sign up for. Meetings every Wednesday morning. There's a notice on the bulletin board. You should take advantage of it.

It's all part of that "load of crap" we fought for and got on behalf of the rest of you people. Me and the other guys on the negotiating team!

CARRIER leaves. MR. MANN feels dreadful.

MR. MANN

Good Lord ... what's happening to me?

He tries to breathe calmly. He leaves his office.

IN THE PARK

MR. MANN has gone to the park to pull himself together.
A WOMAN is taking a walk while pushing a baby carriage.
Another WOMAN is doing tai chi. A JOGGER runs by.
A PARK EMPLOYEE whistles while picking up litter.

MR. MANN sits on a bench. He is very upset about what just
happened at the office. He is completely turned in on himself
and doesn't see the people around him. Doesn't see the trees
or feel the sun. We hear a flock of geese fly overhead.
Everyone except him looks up to watch them. The JOGGER
runs back on, stops, checks his heart rate, does a few
stretches ...

The Chekhov character IRINA enters and sits on the bench
next to MR. MANN.

IRINA

"This morning when I got up and washed, suddenly everything seemed clear to me. Now I know how I ought to live my life. I know. Each of us must work by the sweat of our brow. Work is the meaning of life – its goal, its happiness, and its joy. The worker getting up at dawn to break stones on the highway is happy. So is the shepherd, and the teacher of little children, and the engineer on his train."

She gets up and leaves. MR. MANN stands wanting to
follow her.

MR. MANN

Miss!

> *Three women are browsing for books. The bookstore CLERK*
> *enters with a used copy of* Three Sisters.

CLERK

Excuse me. Sir? This is the only copy I could find. A collection
of two plays: *Uncle Vanya* and *Three Sisters*. When you finish
reading Three *Sisters*, well, you can read the other one. Here.

MR. MANN

Thank you. How much do I owe you?

CLERK

Oh ... that copy isn't in very good shape, so, let's say ... three dollars.
A dollar a sister! You're lucky. It's my last copy. A whole whack of
students came in – it's on right now in town – they had to read it
for class.

MR. MANN

Yes. I went to see it last night.

CLERK

Oh yeah?

MR. MANN

(*handing him the money*) Here you are.

CLERK

Thanks. So did I.

MR. MANN

You saw it?

CLERK

Yes.

MR. MANN

Did you like it?

CLERK

"Oooh ... Moscow, Moscow" ... enough already, right?

MR. MANN

Oh! You ...

CLERK

Between you and me, Chekhov ... I've seen every single Chekhov that's
been produced here in town, and I always feel the same the way. No
matter how good the production is ... the directing ... at some point ...
"Moscow, Moscow ..." Go to Moscow, for Chrissakes! What's stopping
you! Stop whining and complaining, pack your things, and go!

> THE WOMEN *shut their books, put them back on the shelf,*
> *and, slightly annoyed at the clerk, begin to leave the*
> *bookstore.*

CLERK

Did you find what you were looking for?

THE WOMEN

Yes. Thank you.

CLERK

Come again.

THE WOMEN

Yes! Will do.

CLERK

(*turning his attention back to MR. MANN*) What was I saying?

MR. MANN

"Moscow, Moscow ..."

CLERK

Oh right. Take *The Cherry Orchard*, for example. It's very good, but
after three-quarters of an hour: sell the goddamn orchard! "Oh, the
cherry orchard! Our cherry orchard! Look! How beautiful the orchard
is! Our childhood! Our past! Moscow! Moscow! I am a seagull!" Know
what I mean?

MR. MANN

Oh well, I ... I liked it. I'm not as knowledgeable as you, but I liked it. The
actors were good. I don't know ... and there were moments ... insights, I
found very profound. (*indicating the book*) That's why I wanted to ...

CLERK

The aphorisms of the Persian poet Rumi are profound, too, but nobody turns them into a play. I don't deny the man's a genius. That's not it, but ... now, Chekhov's short stories are fabulous. That's what you should read, by the way, but as a playwright, he's a failure. Sublime maybe, but a failure all the same. And, it's bourgeois.

MR. MANN

Oh really?

CLERK

Absolutely! Very bourgeois. They have everything they need but still they're disappointed. They don't know what's wrong: "We should do this, we should do that, but we don't, we change nothing. Nevertheless, we're deeply moved" – and the audience is too. Very, very bourgeois.

MR. MANN

Oh. Okay. So that's bourgeois theatre?

CLERK

Yes.

MR. MANN

Well, thank you. I'll read it anyway and maybe I'll buy the short stories some other time.

CLERK

Sure. Fine. I'm here to help. See you again.

MR. MANN

See you.

He sits on a bench and opens the book.

THE HOSPITAL

A MALE NURSE (the actor who played the JOGGER) hurries past. Another NURSE (the woman doing tai chi) puts away patients' files. MR. MANN is sitting on a chair in the hospital corridor. Still reading. A HOSPITAL JANITOR (the actor who played the PARK EMPLOYEE) sweeps up litter with a broom. A NURSE (the actress who played IRINA) sits down beside

*MR. MANN to tell him that he can now visit his younger
co-worker, SYLVAIN.*

*Another NURSE (the actress who played the woman pushing
the baby carriage) enters with SYLVAIN in a wheelchair.*

SYLVAIN
Hey, hey, hey!

MR. MANN
Well, well, well! What are you doing here?

SYLVAIN
(*trying to get up out of the wheelchair*) I decided to take a bit of a holiday –

NURSE
Don't get up.

SYLVAIN
(*sitting back down*) ... but I didn't want to spend too much money, so
I said to myself, how about a nice relaxing week in the hospital! I'm
already paying for it!

MR. MANN
Definitely a good idea 'cause you're looking great.

SYLVAIN
If it weren't for the food, I think I'd stay another week!

MR. MANN
Oh no you don't! We really miss you at work.

SYLVAIN
Oh yeah! You miss me?

MR. MANN
You bet. There's no one around to make us laugh.

SYLVAIN
Maybe I'll stay another week then!

They laugh.

SYLVAIN
You're the only one from the office who's come to visit me.

MR. MANN
   Really?

SYLVAIN
   Yes.

MR. MANN
   They'll be by, it's just that –

SYLVAIN
   Forget it. It's all right. People are busy.

MR. MANN
   You can say that again! They sent you this card. The whole gang in the
   department. Here.

   MR. MANN hands SYLVAIN a greeting card.

SYLVAIN
   Thank you.

   SYLVAIN reads the card.

MR. MANN
   Don't read what's written down at the bottom there, on the right.

SYLVAIN
   Okay, sure. You on your lunch break right now?

MR. MANN
   No, no. I took the day off. I never take time off! Sick leave. Gotta use it
   sometime, eh!

SYLVAIN
   Take a whole week and come join me! There're some pretty little nurses
   in here, let me tell you!

MR. MANN
   Don't tempt me! (*laughter*) So ... how are you? What's going
   on with you?

SYLVAIN
   Ooh ... I don't know. (*pause*) I've been really tired for quite a while now.
   I don't do a thing and I'm exhausted. Have to kick myself in the butt all
   the time. My girlfriend said to me: "You've got mono. Go see the doctor,

I'm sure you've got mono!" I listened to her and look what happened –
I ended up in here.

MR. MANN

Women! Should never listen to them!

SYLVAIN

You're telling me. Don't know what got into me!

> The two men laugh.

MR. MANN

So ... did they find anything?

SYLVAIN

No. Some old stuff. I've had pneumonia a couple of times. They found
a small spot on one of my lungs. Nothing serious apparently. And
anyway, the doc says they've got plenty of Liquid Paper in this place!

MR. MANN

A little dab'll do ya, right! (*laughter*) Maybe you're anemic. Maybe that's
all it is.

SYLVAIN

Maybe. They found something not quite right with my white
blood cells.

MR. MANN

Why does that not surprise me. You've been going full tilt for quite a
while now: work, two small kids, the cottage – I don't know how many
hours you've spent working on that cottage.

SYLVAIN

If they give me a month off to recuperate, I know where I'll spend it!

MR. MANN

Yeah but not for too long, 'cause the office feels real empty without you.

SYLVAIN

Oh yeah?

MR. MANN

Yeah.

> Pause.

SYLVAIN

I won't be in here long. No such luck. I'll be back to bug you guys next week. You haven't gotten rid of me yet.

The NURSE who dropped him off is back for SYLVAIN now.

NURSE

It's time for your scan.

SYLVAIN

Look how well they treat me in here! They're always smiling! And they don't even want me to walk. Have you ever seen anything like it! It's the first time in my life I've ever let a woman drive me around. See ya!

MR. MANN

See you!

SYLVAIN

Come visit me again. I don't go out much!

MR. MANN goes to the door to watch the NURSE wheel SYLVAIN out of the room. MR. MANN goes back and sits down. He has a bad feeling about all this – a presentiment. Three nurses walk by laughing. A MALE NURSE picks up a chair close to MR. MANN to move it elsewhere.

MALE NURSE

Excuse me.

He leaves. A YOUNG MAN dressed in street clothes, smoking a cigarette, approaches MR. MANN.

YOUNG MAN

Is someone sitting here?

MR. MANN

No.

YOUNG MAN

Thank you.

The YOUNG MAN takes the chair and goes to sit a little ways off. MR. MANN goes back to reading his book.

The waitress, ANITA, enters moving to the music playing in the café. She goes from table to table taking people's orders or serving them. MR. MANN is lost in his book.

To one side, the woman DIRECTOR of the Three Sisters *production is being interviewed by a young REPORTER from the university newspaper. MR. MANN doesn't notice her. On the other side, two friends, a YOUNG MAN and CATHYA, discuss a project. She's a visual artist; he's a possible sponsor.*

ANITA places an espresso on the table in front of MR. MANN.

ANITA

Your espresso.

MR. MANN

Thank you.

He follows her with his eyes as she moves about the café.

DIRECTOR

There's often a kind of synchronicity when you're directing a play. For example, with *Three Sisters*, a number of things happened to me which had a direct link with the play.

ANITA approaches the table where the DIRECTOR and the REPORTER are seated.

ANITA

Everything good here?

DIRECTOR

Yes, thanks.

ANITA

Still don't want anything?

REPORTER

No, I'm fine. Thank you.

DIRECTOR

A program on the radio, a conversation, a piece of music. It was as if they happened in answer to a question I'd been asking myself.

CATHYA

I was thinking five hundred dollars.

YOUNG MAN

Five hundred!

CATHYA

Yeah but you'd get a full-page ad in the program. It'd be really good publicity for you.

YOUNG MAN

How many people will come to your show? A hundred? Two hundred?

CATHYA

Lots of people will come.

YOUNG MAN

Hey, Anita, would you sponsor an art exhibit on snow? She's asking me for five hundred dollars.

CATHYA

It's an installation, not an exhibit.

ANITA

With the kind of money you're making, you should give her a thousand.

ANITA and CATHYA laugh together.

YOUNG MAN

Hey, come on!

ANITA

Quit stalling and show some support for the arts! Her work is really beautiful!

YOUNG MAN

Okay, all right, five hundred.

MR. MANN stirs his coffee. Time passes.

*Two YOUNG MEN at one table are eyeing two YOUNG
WOMEN at another. The men seem to be hatching a plan.
ANITA brings them their drinks.*

YOUNG MAN 1

Anita, see those two young women over there. We want to pay for
their drinks.

*ANITA laughs and then crosses over to the two YOUNG
WOMEN, but YOUNG MAN 1 calls out to her.*

YOUNG MAN 1

Anita! Wait a sec!

*He takes off his wedding band. They laugh. MR. MANN
watches them and follows the goings-on with amusement. As
she crosses over to the YOUNG WOMEN, she leaves another
coffee on his table.*

ANITA

Here you go.

MR. MANN

Thank you.

She approaches the two YOUNG WOMEN.

YOUNG WOMAN 1

Thanks, Anita. We'll pay you now.

ANITA

No, no. It's already been taken care of by those two gentlemen
over there.

*They look across. The two YOUNG MEN wave. The two
YOUNG WOMEN laugh. As ANITA turns away, one of
the two YOUNG WOMEN calls her back.*

YOUNG WOMAN 1

Anita, do you know them?

ANITA
A little.

YOUNG WOMAN 2
And?

ANITA
Not all that great!

> *They laugh. The two YOUNG WOMEN raise their glasses to the two YOUNG MEN who, proud of themselves, return the gesture. MR. MANN smiles at all this. ANITA gives him a wink as though they know something the others don't. He goes back to his book.*

> *MR. MANN stirs his coffee. Time passes.*

> *Now, over to one side, four friends are deep in conversation. They are university students. BOY 2 and GIRL 2 are a couple. There's also an empty table with used coffee cups. MR. MANN is still very much absorbed in his book.*

BOY 1
They're all a bunch of hicks, up north there.

GIRL 1
Oh come on. You're being such a fascist!

BOY 1
It's true!

GIRL 2
You're living proof that a master's degree doesn't mean a thing.

BOY 1
Look, the government throws money out the window funding make-work projects so those people can stay back there in the bush with the bears.

GIRL 1 and GIRL 2
Oh! Come on!

BOY 2

It's true. Face it. The remote regions of this province are good for one
thing and one thing only – natural resources. That's it.

GIRL 2

(*to BOY 2, her boyfriend*) You don't agree with him! You're just saying
the first thing that pops into your head. Please.

GIRL 1

(*to BOY 1*) Where are you from anyway?

BOY 1

Abitibi.

GIRL 1 and GIRL 2

I knew it! Ha!

BOY 1

I didn't stay there, did I? I'm not stupid.

GIRL 1

There's more to this province than Montreal.

BOY 1

Oh yeah? Tell me. What real fun can you have if you *don't* live
in Montreal?

GIRL 2

Montreal, Montreal!

BOY 1

Yeah right ... Moscow, Moscow! I got it, Miss Ph.D.

GIRL 1

Well, I'm heading back home as soon as I finish school.

BOY 2

Where are you from, Anita?

ANITA

Baie-Comeau.

GIRL 1 and GIRL 2

There! You see!

BOY 1

    Ah, but she didn't stay, did she! Anita's a smart girl. Would
    you go back?

ANITA

    If I had a steady boyfriend, to start a family, I might.

BOY 1

    Okay. I could make an exception for Baie-Comeau ... and you, Anita.

ANITA

    Sweet-talker!

BOY 2

    I could too! Maybe I could join the two of you?

ANITA

    Promises, promises!

       ANITA brings MR. MANN another cup of coffee. The
       conversation at the table of friends continues, but it fades
       slowly, so we hear them less and less.

GIRL 2

    (*to BOY 2, her boyfriend*) Yeah. Well ... good thing for you I'm not
    easily offended!

GIRL 1

    Christ, you guys can be such jerks. (*exits*)

       ANITA serves MR. MANN another cup of coffee.

ANITA

    A decaf.

MR. MANN

    Thank you.

ANITA

    Are they disturbing you? I can ask them to tone it down, if you like?

MR. MANN

    No, no. Thank you. You're very kind.

ANITA clears the empty table. MR. MANN watches her work.
He is completely taken with this woman, by the joy she exudes.
This troubles him though. ANITA goes back to the kitchen and
MR. MANN to his book. The conversation among the three
friends (BOY 1, BOY 2, and GIRL 2) has taken a more
serious turn.

BOY 2

Come on, the environment, per se, doesn't exist!

GIRL 2

What do you mean, it doesn't exist!

BOY 2

It doesn't exist. It's the Green lobby trying to get grants and increase
their funding.

GIRL 2

Oh come on! I think I'm going to sleep at my place tonight!

BOY 2

Do whatever you like! Do you really think the multinationals are going
to lay the planet to waste? They're not crazy! It's their market. They're
not going to shoot themselves in the foot!

GIRL 2

There isn't a single source of pure water left anywhere on earth. There's
smog, massive climate change, expanding deserts, epidemics. Hello! Is
that what you call taking care of your market?

BOY 2

Technology will solve all that. I've explained it to you.

BOY 1

Things go in cycles. There used to be palm trees in Antarctica. You've
got to be zen about it.

GIRL 2

Yeah but that's no help when you're trying to decide whether to have
children or not.

BOY 2

Why have children? There are too many people on the planet as it is.

MR. MANN is more and more absorbed by his reading. Lights on the three friends (BOY 1, BOY 2, and GIRL 2) start to fade. The last lines are in decrescendo. MR. MANN continues to read. Time passes.

Of the two couples, only one is left in the café (BOY 2 and GIRL 2). They're silent. Clearly, the conversation has not gone well. NICOLE, the newspaper vendor, enters.

NICOLE

Hi.

ANITA

Hello.

NICOLE

Can I, eh ...

ANITA

Sure. I'll bring you a cup right away.

NICOLE

I don't want to bother you.

ANITA

No, no. No problem.

NICOLE goes and sits at a table. MR. MANN looks up at her. She waves at him. ANITA comes back with a coffee and sets it in front of NICOLE.

ANITA

Here.

NICOLE

Thanks. You're so nice.

ANITA

Did you sell much today?

NICOLE

No, not much. (*She takes a sip of her coffee.*) Hmm! Coffee's good. Nice and strong!

> MOMO *enters.*

ANITA

Look who's here! My boyfriend!

MOMO

My love! (*He gives her a big hug.*) D'you wanna marry me?

ANITA

You know you're the only man for me!

MOMO

My love!

ANITA

Want a small juice?

MOMO

A big one. I want a real big one.

NICOLE

Go wait for me at my spot.

MOMO

What?

NICOLE

Go wait for me at my spot. What if someone comes by.

MOMO

Relax, Nicole! I'm thirsty.

NICOLE

Drink your drink and get over there.

MOMO

Prends soin!

> ANITA *hands MOMO a drink.*

ANITA

Here.

MOMO

What is it?

ANITA

Apple.

MOMO

A big juicy apple! (*He drinks.*) Oh that's good! I don't like grapefruit
though. It stings. (*pointing to MR. MANN*) That man, who is he?

ANITA

A customer.

MOMO

I don't know him.

ANITA

He's new.

MOMO

A new customer! (*As he leaves, he looks up at the top of the doorframe.*)
The bell isn't there anymore?

ANITA

No, it's gone.

MOMO

It's gone south! See ya! *Prends soin!*

> ANITA laughs. MOMO leaves. ANITA goes over to the window
> and looks out, waiting. NICOLE drinks her hot cup of coffee.
> MR. MANN reads. Pause. Suddenly, BOY 2 gets up and puts
> money on the table. He leaves. GIRL 2 puts her head in her
> hands. MR. MANN and ANITA look at her. Pause. MR. MANN
> goes back to his book.

MR. MANN

"Oh, listen to the music! They're leaving us ... one of them is gone for
good ... forever! We're left alone ... to start our lives all over again."

GIRL 2

(*trying to pull herself together*) "We must go on living ... must go
on living."

NICOLE

Spring will be over soon. Then it'll be summer and I'm gonna die of heat at that corner but I'll go on working and working.

ANITA

"Someday, I hope, we'll know what the purpose of all this suffering is ... if only we knew."

NICOLE

"If only we knew."

MR. MANN

"Nothing matters?"

GIRL 2

"If only we knew."

MR. MANN

"Nothing matters!"

ANITA

(*as she exits*) "If only we knew."

Finished reading, MR. MANN closes the book.

DINNER

It's the end of the evening meal. The whole family is at the table. They're having dessert and coffee. CLAUDETTE stands.

CLAUDETTE

Listen up, everyone. We're celebrating tonight!

MR. MANN

What are we celebrating?

CLAUDETTE

I bought a bottle of good port.

NADINE

Great! What's the occasion?

CLAUDETTE

We're celebrating the sale of that damn house.

Exclamations except for QUENTIN.

NADINE and MR. MANN
You sold it?!

CLAUDETTE
No such luck, but I'm pretending I did. I kept doing those visualization exercises – you know, visualizing I'm selling it. That didn't work. So I decided to act like it's sold. Maybe that'll work.

MR. MANN
Okay ... maybe it will!

NADINE
You're going to sell it, Mom.

CLAUDETTE
Oh, I don't know. It'd been getting me down.

NADINE
Don't get discouraged.

MR. MANN
You're going to sell it, Claudette ...

QUENTIN
Sure you will. At some point.

CLAUDETTE
Cheers.

EVERYONE
Yes, cheers. Yes. Cheers. Cheers.

CLAUDETTE
Hmm, this is a very nice port.

I've been thinking. I want to change market. Of house, I mean. I'm fed up with starter homes. If I could break into the luxury-home bracket ... Sell ten a year and you're laughing all the way to the bank. And, you've got time to enjoy life. Do you want to know what I dream of doing? Okay. It's just a dream, but do you want to know what it is?

MR. MANN and NADINE
Sure.

CLAUDETTE

I want to buy an apartment block. A really nice one. There are a few I've got my eye on in Lower Town not far from the market. They're great. Not too expensive. I'd buy a building with six apartments. We'd keep one for ourselves. One for Nadine and one for Quentin. And rent out the rest.

NADINE

Great idea!

CLAUDETTE

We'd each have our own space. We wouldn't be getting in each other's way all the time. You two could do what you want, decorate the way you want.

NADINE

That'd be fantastic!

MR. MANN

What would we do with the house?

CLAUDETTE

Sell it.

MR. MANN

Oh ... but ... all the work's done on it now. I've completely renovated it. It's finally just the way we want it. And it's paid for.

CLAUDETTE

Exactly. A house without a dream is a dead house. That's a Chinese proverb, I think.

This port is really very, very good. A young couple came by the other day when I was out front on the lawn. They wanted to know if the house was for sale. And I said to myself, why not? It's close to all the schools, which is of no use to us anymore – Nadine's at university and Quentin's stopped going. We could sell this house like that!

MR. MANN

Let's talk about it some other time.

CLAUDETTE

Of course, this is all just pie-in-the-sky right now. But we have to start thinking about it. The kids will only be here a little while longer – Quentin until he figures out what he's doing with his life and Nadine ... Oh, Nadine! Did you tell your father?

NADINE

I passed my German exam! I'm going to register for the summer session and take a fourth language.

MR. MANN

Congratulations!

NADINE

Thank you.

QUENTIN

What good is knowing how to speak German in Quebec City?

CLAUDETTE

There's more to life than Quebec City, Quentin. You've got to leave the village. In this day and age, a person can't know too many languages.

NADINE

I want to take four courses this summer so I can finish my B.A. in two and a half years.

CLAUDETTE

Isn't she fantastic?! You impress me so much, Nadine.

MR. MANN

Don't you feel like taking some time off this summer? Enjoy life a little?

NADINE

I am, Dad. I like studying. I want to get my doctorate as quickly as possible so you won't have to –

CLAUDETTE

Nadine, your father and I have told you –

MR. MANN

That's right. We'll be here for you as long as you want to study.

NADINE

It's just that I've got five, six years left, easy.

MR. MANN

As long as you need, honey.

NADINE

Thank you. (*turning to her brother*) Quentin, I saw Claude the other day; he said you hadn't been by with your CV.

QUENTIN

Haven't had time. I've had other things to do.

NADINE

Okay, but if you wait too long the job'll be gone. I've told you, all you have to do is say you're my brother and they'll hire you.

QUENTIN

You and your goddamn CV. I'll drop it off, okay!

CLAUDETTE

No swearing at the table.

NADINE

It's not *my* CV.

QUENTIN

Look, I've got other plans.

NADINE

Which won't work out. They never do.

CLAUDETTE

That's true, Quentin. How long have you been looking for something? You can't go on living off the odd jobs you do for us around the house.

MR. MANN

Give him a chance. He'll go. He said he'd go and he will! Right, Quentin? You're going to go?

QUENTIN

Sure.

MR. MANN

Okay. And I'm the one who asked him to work on the trellis. You did a very good job, by the way. Thank you, Quentin.

CLAUDETTE

Anyway ... what can I say? Quentin's always been like that. Always have to push him. No get-up-and-go. Can't get moving on his own.

NADINE

It's just that you keep saying you're looking for work. If you don't want to go –

QUENTIN

I'll go!

MR. MANN

We've discussed this. It's settled. Now, let's drop it.

> *Pause.*

CLAUDETTE

Oh, Nadine, I've been meaning to tell you, I ran into Bernard Couture. Guess what. His son's in languages too. And do you know what he's doing now? He's an interpreter at the House of Commons in Ottawa.

NADINE

Oh yeah?

CLAUDETTE

Yep. Now I think they're absolutely amazing! I don't know how they do it.

NADINE

Takes practice. You get used to it. (*starts to clear the dinner dishes*)

CLAUDETTE

They listen to the other person and, while that person is talking, they keep listening and translate as they go.

NADINE

Takes practice. You get used to it.

CLAUDETTE

That means they have to speak almost without thinking. I don't know how they do it!

MR. MANN looks at QUENTIN, who's staring at the floor.

NADINE

Takes practice. You eating your dessert?

CLAUDETTE

No, you can have it. Take the people who translate for heads of state. Imagine how brilliant they have to be!

NADINE eats her mother's dessert.

NADINE

I suppose.

CLAUDETTE

You see them standing there. Right behind. They can't afford to make a mistake! Can you imagine how much they have to know! All sorts of stuff we don't. I could see you doing something like that. You'd be good at it. (*daydreaming about it*) Oh yeah ... really good ...

MR. MANN looks at them all and suddenly "sees" his family: his son, hunched over, with his eyes on the floor; his daughter, wolfing down her mother's dessert; his wife sipping her wine. ANDREY, from Three Sisters, *crosses the stage.*

ANDREY

"Oh, where has my past gone? Where has it disappeared? I was young and carefree and clever. I used to have fine dreams, great thoughts, and the present and the future were bright with hope ... Why do we become so dull and commonplace and uninteresting almost before we've begun to live? Why do we become lazy, indifferent, useless, unhappy? And all this overwhelming vulgarity and pettiness crushes our children and extinguishes any spark they might have in them, so that they, too, become miserable, half-dead creatures the same as each other and the same as their parents." (*exits*)

Shift.

CLAUDETTE

Yoo-hoo! What do you think?

MR. MANN

(*snapping out of his reverie*) What! Uh ... yes, Moscow, that's a good idea.

    Amazed silence.

CLAUDETTE

What did you say?

MR. MANN

Oh, uh ... all I said was ...

CLAUDETTE

Moscow?

QUENTIN

Connection, Dad?

MR. MANN

Oh. I was thinking about the play I saw the other day. I was a million miles away.

CLAUDETTE

Oh.

MR. MANN

Which reminds me, I was thinking of going back tonight.

CLAUDETTE

Going back where?

MR. MANN

To see the play.

CLAUDETTE

You went last week.

MR. MANN

Yes, but ... I really liked it and I want to go see it again.

CLAUDETTE

Go back a second time!

MR. MANN

Yes, go back a second time. What? I'm not allowed to or something?

CLAUDETTE

No, no, you're allowed. But you could've mentioned it to me.

MR. MANN

Do you want to come? I haven't bought the tickets yet.

CLAUDETTE

No, I can't tonight. There's a house I have to –

MR. MANN

Okay, fine. You won't be here. Nadine is going to Hugo's and Quentin? ... Quentin will be over at Latch's. So I might as well go to the theatre instead of spending the evening in front of the TV.

CLAUDETTE

What's gotten into you? You're awfully cranky tonight.

MR. MANN

I'm not cranky! All I did was say I wanted to go to the theatre and you're making a big deal out of it.

> *NADINE and QUENTIN leave the room as quietly as they possibly can.*

CLAUDETTE

Oh come on! I'm not! It's just that you've never done something like that before – go see a play twice. It's only normal I'm a little surprised, that's all.

MR. MANN

Okay, fine, if you don't want me to go, I won't! I'll clean up the dishes and you three go about your business!

CLAUDETTE

(*mimicking*) He's not cranky! Go if you want to go! You're not a prisoner. All I'm saying is that I find it strange you didn't tell me about it.

MR. MANN

Maybe I should've mentioned it but I was sure that –

CLAUDETTE

All right, it's okay, I understand. Go to the theatre! (*She starts to leave but stops and turns.*) Are you sure that's all this is?

MR. MANN
    What?

CLAUDETTE
    Are you sure it's just because you like the play?

MR. MANN
    Yes. What else would it be?

CLAUDETTE
    I don't know. I'm asking *you*. Are you sure there isn't something else?

MR. MANN
    No.

        MR. MANN leaves home for the theatre.

AT THE THEATRE

        *MR. MANN takes a seat in the theatre. A man enters and sits
        down. Then, ANITA enters followed by another WOMAN.
        MR. MANN and ANITA suddenly notice each other.*

ANITA
    Oh, hello!

MR. MANN
    Hello.

ANITA
    I hope your stomach isn't bothering you too much.

MR. MANN
    What ...?

ANITA
    Well ... with all the cups of coffee you drank at the café this afternoon.

MR. MANN
    Oh! No, no, I'm fine.

        Another MAN enters and takes a seat.

ANITA
    You're to blame, you know.

MR. MANN
    For what?

ANITA
    If I'm here. I saw you reading the play and I hadn't had time to go see it
    yet ... so –

MR. MANN
    Oh! Well ... good.

        *Another woman arrives and goes and sits next to the first
        man. They are HUSBAND and WIFE.*

WIFE
    I'm sorry. The meeting was interminable. Finally, I had to say I had
    tickets for the theatre. Otherwise I'd still be there.

HUSBAND
    That's okay.

        The house lights dim.

ANITA
    Hope you enjoy it.

MR. MANN
    Thank you. You too.

        We hear the opening music.

HUSBAND
    You'll never guess what Laroche did today?

WIFE
    No.

HUSBAND
    Well ... he had vertical blinds in his office –

        People around them signal the couple to be quiet.

HUSBAND
    I'll tell you later.

        *We hear the opening music and the WIFE unwrapping a
        candy. Sighs of exasperation from a few of the audience
        members. The play begins. Again, the actors recreate*

characters from Three Sisters, *but this time the actors remain
seated. They are both audience and characters in the play.*

ACTRESS PLAYING NADINE

"When I woke up this morning, and after I got up and washed, I
suddenly felt as if everything in the world had become clear to me, and
I knew how I ought to live. Every man must work by the sweat of his
brow. That should be the whole meaning and purpose of his life, his
happiness, and his joy."

ACTOR PLAYING SYLVAIN

"Time will pass and we will leave this earth forever. We will be
forgotten. Our voices, our faces, will be forgotten."

ACTOR PLAYING QUENTIN

"The geese, for example, they fly on and on without knowing why
or where they're going. And, what does it matter, as long as they go
on flying."

ACTRESS PLAYING CLAUDETTE

"All the same, what is the meaning of it all?"

ACTOR PLAYING QUENTIN

"The meaning ...? Look out there. It's snowing. What's the meaning
of that?"

ACTRESS PLAYING CLAUDETTE

"But there has to be some meaning to life?"

ACTRESS PLAYING ANITA

(*standing*) "When you have to take your happiness in snatches, in small
doses, as I do, and then lose it, as I've lost it, you gradually get hardened
and bad-tempered." (*She sits.*)

ACTOR PLAYING QUENTIN

(*standing*) "Oh, all this longing for work. How well I understand it!
I've never done a stroke of work in my life. I was born in Petersburg,
an unfriendly and idle city – born into a family where work and
worry were completely unknown. I remember a valet pulling off my
boots for me when I came home from cadet school, and my mother
looked on in admiration. But the time's come: something enormous
is heading our way, a terrific storm which will blow away all this

idleness and indifference and prejudice against work, this rot of boredom that our society is suffering from. I'm going to work, and in twenty-five or thirty years' time every man and woman will be working. Every single one of us!" (*He sits.*)

MR. MANN

(*standing up*) Excuse me, Mr. Tuzenbach, but I don't agree with what you just said. Yes, you're right that everyone started to work, everyone works, but it's not true that it's brought us happiness. I've been working since I was twenty and, as time goes by, I have to work harder and harder. Everyone around me is working more and more. Some even fall sick from overwork. But no one is any the happier for it. That's not the secret. That's not it. Your play is very beautiful but, there, at that point, the play is wrong. The playwright is mistaken. A hundred years later everyone will be working, that's true, and everyone will be richer but nothing will have changed, everyone will be just as unhappy!

> *He sits down again. The play ends. Everyone stands to applaud. Everyone except MR. MANN, who takes a moment to react.*

> *The audience leaves the theatre.*

WIFE

So, what were you saying about Laroche?

HUSBAND

He had them taken down and installed an air conditioner.

> *Their conversation fades as they leave. MR. MANN and ANITA meet up.*

ANITA

It was good, eh? Did you like it?

MR. MANN

Oh yes! Very much. Very, very much.

ANITA

It's beautiful. Isn't it.

MR. MANN

Yes. All those love stories ... unhappy love stories ... their need for love, I find it all very beautiful, very moving.

ANITA

That's true. There's so much in that play. So many layers.

MR. MANN

Yes. Maybe it's just a little bourgeois though.

ANITA

Bourgeois? You think?

MR. MANN

Ah ... me, personally? No. But I've heard some people say that.

ANITA

Who?

MR. MANN

Well ... people "in the know."

ANITA

People "in the know" often don't get what people like you and me are talking about!

They laugh.

MR. MANN

That's possible. I don't know enough to judge. This is the second time I've seen the play, and I liked it even more this time.

ANITA

Really!

MR. MANN

Yes. I think I could see it many more times and I wouldn't tire of it.

ANITA

Well, I'll tell them. They'll be very happy to hear it. They're friends of mine.

MR. MANN

Really!

ANITA

Yes.

MR. MANN

They're your friends?!

ANITA

Yep. They rehearsed at the café. They didn't have much money so they'd rehearse at night. The tables and chairs in the play are from the café.

MR. MANN

Really!

ANITA

Yes.

MR. MANN

Well, it was worth it. Please congratulate them for me.

ANITA

Come tell them yourself. I'm sure it would make them very happy.

MR. MANN

(*hesitating*) No, no ... I have to get home. I've got to be at work early tomorrow morning.

ANITA

Okay. (*pause*) Well ... see you again, maybe.

MR. MANN

Yes. Yes, for sure. Good night.

> *ANITA goes backstage. We hear the offstage voices of her friends in the dressing room. We hear exclamations when she enters; then a few snippets of their conversation. MR. MANN listens.*

OFFSTAGE VOICES

– Hey! Anita!

– I knew you were in the audience!

– We recognized your laugh.

– I spotted her, but I forgot to tell you.

ANITA

Bravo! You guys were very good.

OFFSTAGE VOICE

Thanks. You liked it?

ANITA

A lot.

OFFSTAGE VOICES

– Did you notice I forgot my lines at one point?

Laughter.

– He did. Way to go, champ.

– Yeah, bravo!

ANITA

It didn't show. There's a man who asked me to tell you how much he liked the show. This is the second time he's seen it.

OFFSTAGE VOICES

– Really!

– Hey, let's go for a drink tonight.

– Yes!

– Not me. I'm rehearsing early tomorrow morning.

– Oh come on.

– No. Saturday.

– Come on!

– No, I'm working.

– Aaaah!

OFFSTAGE VOICES

– (*quoting a line from the play*) "It's too bad, all the same, that our youth has slipped so quickly away."

Laughter.

On these last words, MR. MANN leaves the theatre.

AFTER THE THEATRE

On the bus going home, MR. MANN notices MOMO and NICOLE. She has her eyes closed and her head is resting on her friend's shoulder. She has a few issues of Outreach *on her lap. The newspapers start sliding off and fall to the floor. NICOLE wakes up. MOMO gathers the newspapers for her.*

MOMO

Prends soin.

NICOLE

Thanks.

> *NICOLE places the papers back on her knees and then yawns.*
> *A huge yawn. It's as though she were silently screaming.*
> *MOMO keeps smiling. They are like the comedy and tragedy*
> *masks of theatre. The bus stops.*

NICOLE

Come on. This is our stop.

> *They get off. MR. MANN watches them.*

MOMO

I'm tired. *Outreach! Outreach!*

NICOLE

Forget the paper, Momo. It's late. My feet hurt.

MOMO

But I like saying it. *Outreach! Outreach!*

> *They leave. MR. MANN watches them go.*

AT HOME

> *Now MR. MANN is at home. He looks around the house.*
> *Suddenly, he feels hot. He takes off his jacket. He opens the*
> *windows. We hear a flock of geese fly over. He watches them*
> *and then sits down on the couch. He turns on the TV and*
> *changes channels. There's nothing interesting on. He turns*
> *it off. Pause. Very softly, we begin to hear the sounds of the*
> *neighbour's lovemaking. He puts his head in his hands. A*
> *man and a woman appear at the window. They are IRINA*
> *and CHEBUTYKIN from* Three Sisters.

CHEBUTYKIN

"Perhaps I'm not a man at all, but I just imagine I've got hands and
feet and a head. It could be I don't exist, and only imagine I'm walking
about and eating and sleeping. Oh, if only I could stop existing!"

> *The neighbour's moans and sighs have changed to sobs.*

IRINA

"I'm forgetting. Every day I'm forgetting more and more, and life's slipping by, and it will never, ever come back ... We shall never go to Moscow ... I can see now that we shall never go."

The man and the woman at the window have disappeared and MR. MANN is left sitting on the sofa with his head still in his hands.

THE HOSPITAL

MR. MANN is sitting alone. A NURSE comes to speak with him. He nods in agreement and then he enters SYLVAIN's hospital room. SYLVAIN is lying in bed. He appears to be much weaker than before.

MR. MANN

Hey! Hey! They changed your room.

SYLVAIN

Oh. Hiya! Yeah they did.

MR. MANN

You're going to be more comfortable here on your own. Nice big room. And will you look at the view! You're at the same level as the trees. It's beautiful.

SYLVAIN

Yes. Did you notice?

MR. MANN

What.

SYLVAIN

The trees.

MR. MANN

What about the trees?

SYLVAIN

Those two, there.

MR. MANN

The maples.

SYLVAIN

Yes. A silver maple and a sugar maple. It's funny, my land up at the cottage is covered with them but I've never really noticed how different they are.

MR. MANN

You're right. The leaves.

SYLVAIN

Not just the leaves, the bark, the branches, everything. They're really very different. Even the leaves don't move the same way-in the wind.

MR. MANN

You're right. Will you look at that. The undersides of the leaves are showing. Bad weather's on the way.

SYLVAIN

It's funny ... it's funny, isn't it, how small, unimportant details can suddenly become very important in life. It's as if I'm seeing those maples for the first time. As if they were looking at me or waiting for me. Aren't they beautiful! Oh, I bet it feels great to ... well, to just "be" alongside trees like that!

MR. MANN

You're going to go to your cottage this summer, Sylvain. I know it. And you're going to have plenty of good times in the shade of your maple trees. Hey, do you realize, I still haven't been to your cottage! After all these years.

SYLVAIN

No, you haven't.

MR. MANN

Every summer, we say we're going to drop by for a visit and, before you know it, the holidays are over and we haven't done a thing about it.

SYLVAIN

We're all the same.

> MR. MANN continues to speak as a NURSE slowly wheels SYLVAIN's hospital bed offstage.

MR. MANN

All right, let's settle this once and for all. Eh? What d'ya say? This summer, we're going to go for sure. You always take the last two in July and the first two in August, right? We haven't decided what we're doing yet. So, okay! The first of August we'll be there! You'll give me the grand tour, I hope. Right? What d'ya say? August first. And you'll show me your famous tool shed! Believe me, we're looking forward to you getting back to the office. Take all the time you need to get better, but we're anxious to have you back. I'm swamped right now with all the work I have to do on the restructuring. It's absolutely crazy. Maybe I could dump some on your desk. Just a little. Look, I should be going. You rest. We're all thinking of you, Sylvain. The whole bunch of us. You get better and come back as soon as you can. Your office is waiting for you. I'll drop by for another little visit later this week. Okay? This week. Well, guess I'll be going. See you. Bye, my friend.

SYLVAIN is no longer there. MR. MANN is filled with deep sadness.

MR. MANN exits to the street. There are no passersby. We hear the sound of a helicopter flying overhead. He walks along. He doesn't want to go home right away. He spots ANITA through the café window and decides to go in.

THE CAFÉ

MR. MANN sits at a table. ANITA almost immediately serves him a cup of coffee. Music plays in the background.

ANITA

There you go.

MR. MANN

Thank you.

He stirs his coffee. She watches him. She sees how sad he is. Pause.

ANITA

Would you like a nice piece of maple sugar pie?

MR. MANN

No, thank you.

ANITA

It's my mother's recipe. It's very comforting.

MR. MANN

I don't doubt it but I'm not partial to sweets.

ANITA

If you change your mind ...

> *She goes back to the table where her three young friends are sitting: JEFF, an ACTOR, and an ACTRESS. Their conversation is very lively and full of fun while MR. MANN sits there thinking about Sylvain.*

ACTOR

I say my line and cross to the door. The door's stuck! I can't open it! So, I give it a good shove. It opens –

ACTRESS

And no one's there!

ACTOR

He decided to make his entrance through the wings instead.

> *Laughter all around.*

ACTRESS

It was awful!

ANITA

Who was it?

ACTOR and ACTRESS

Vincent!

> *More laughter.*

ACTOR

Oh, Anita. This is Jeff. He's a friend from theatre school. We go way back.

> *JEFF stands and shakes ANITA's hand.*

JEFF

Hi.

ANITA

Hi.

ACTOR

Jeff went back home to Gaspé after school, but I've finally persuaded him to leave. He's going to replace me in the show.

ANITA

Oh really! You're quitting?

ACTOR

Well no, but we got an offer to do a festival in France.

ACTRESS

And if that goes well maybe we'll tour.

ANITA

That's so great!

ACTRESS

It is, isn't it?!

ACTOR

It's great but it's in August and I'm doing another show. Let's just say it was bad good news for me. Anyway, it'll all work out; Jeff's a really good actor.

JEFF

Who am I playing?

ACTOR

Tuzenbach. I didn't tell you?

JEFF

You must've, but I was so excited when you called that I forgot everything. I haven't acted for four years. Tuzenbach is the one who ...

ACTRESS

He's the baron in love with Irina.

JEFF

Right! The one who keeps saying he's going to go to work but never does.

ACTRESS

That's him.

JEFF

Okay. And you're playing Irina?

ACTRESS

That's right.

ANITA goes to the window, waiting.

ACTOR

Good. Hmm ... Today, we'll go through the play but we'll only read the scenes between Irina and Tuzenbach. I'll talk to you about the character as we go. We'll get that done at least.

JEFF

Okay.

ACTOR

All right, aah ... It's Irina's birthday. There's lots of people, lots of activity. Everyone's running around. Then, at one point, the two of you find yourselves alone together. Okay, let's start.

JEFF

"What are you thinking about?"

ACTRESS

"Oh nothing. I don't like that fellow Solyony."

Slowly, MR. MANN looks at ANITA. The music and the ambience in the café start to change.

JEFF

"He's a strange man. I think he's shy. You're twenty years old and I'm not thirty yet. We still have many, many years ahead of us."

ACTRESS

"Don't talk to me about love."

ANITA looks at MR. MANN.

JEFF

"I long so passionately for life, Irina, and because, by some miracle, you are beautiful, life also appears beautiful to me!"

ANITA walks towards him.

JEFF

"My treasure! You seem more beautiful every day! What wonderful, beautiful hair! What marvellous eyes! But – there's only one "but," only one – you don't love me!"

ACTRESS

"I can't help that. I've never loved anyone in my life."

JEFF

"Such trifles, such silly little things sometimes become so important suddenly for no apparent reason. It's as though I were seeing those fir trees and maples and birches for the very first time in my life. They seem to be looking at me with a certain curiosity, waiting for something. What beautiful trees! And how beautiful, when you think of it, life ought to be with trees like these in it! Ah well. And if I die, it seems to me that I shall still have a share of life somehow or other. Irina!"

ACTRESS

"What?"

JEFF

"I didn't have my coffee this morning. Will you tell them to get some ready for me?"

ACTOR

Yes. That's it. That was very good.

JEFF

I'll reread the play tonight after seeing the show. Not to worry.

ACTOR and ACTRESS

We're not.

ACTOR

All right! We've got to go. I reserved a ticket for you near the front.

JEFF

Perfect. I'm really glad you called me because – well, *Three Sisters* is my favourite Chekhov.

JEFF

"My treasure! You seem more beautiful every day! What wonderful, beautiful hair! What marvellous eyes! But – there's only one "but," only one – you don't love me!"

ACTRESS

"I can't help that. I've never loved anyone in my life."

JEFF

"Such trifles, such silly little things sometimes become so important suddenly for no apparent reason. It's as though I were seeing those fir trees and maples and birches for the very first time in my life. They seem to be looking at me with a certain curiosity, waiting for something. What beautiful trees! And how beautiful, when you think of it, life ought to be with trees like these in it! Ah well. And if I die, it seems to me that I shall still have a share of life somehow or óther. Irina!"

ACTRESS

"What?"

JEFF

"I didn't have my coffee this morning. Will you tell them to get some ready for me?"

ACTOR

Yes. That's it. That was very good.

JEFF

I'll reread the play tonight after seeing the show. Not to worry.

ACTOR AND ACTRESS

We're not.

ACTOR

All right! We've got to go. I reserved a ticket for you near the front.

JEFF

Perfect. I'm really glad you called me because – well, *Three Sisters* is my favourite Chekhov.

ACTOR
Really?

JEFF
Yeah, somehow it's a play about living in a rural area far from the centre, you know ...

ACTOR
Uh ... yeah ... well, you should talk to Martine about that. She'll be there tonight.

ACTRESS
Anita! Put it on our tab, okay.

> *The actors leave. MR. MANN gets up to pay and to leave as well. ANITA crosses over to his table.*

MR. MANN
Here.

ANITA .
Thanks.

MR. MANN
No. You keep it.

ANITA
Goodness! Well, thank you.

MR. MANN
It's for the pie ...

ANITA
My pleasure ... are you going back to see the play tonight?

MR. MANN
No.

ANITA
Have a nice evening.

MR. MANN
Thank you. You too.

MR. MANN is at home. ANITA can still be seen in the café all through this scene.

CLAUDETTE
Hello.

MR. MANN
Hello.

CLAUDETTE
Come sit down.

MR. MANN
I was just at the hospital.

CLAUDETTE
I didn't ask you where you'd been.

MR. MANN
I know. I went to see Sylvain.

CLAUDETTE
Sylvain ...?

MR. MANN
From the office.

CLAUDETTE
Oh yeah. The "joker." The one who built himself a tool shed out of the bottoms of empty wine bottles.

MR. MANN
And he drank every one of them. Yeah. He won't be drinking too many more.

CLAUDETTE
Oh no.

Silence.

MR. MANN
Thirty-two years old. Two little boys.

CLAUDETTE
Has he been sick long?

MR. MANN

No. Seems as though it's been one after the other lately. Around us, I mean. Bruno over Christmas. Jean-Guy last year. Our turn next, I guess.

　·　*Silence.*

CLAUDETTE

Is that what's been making you sad? You've been sad lately.

MR. MANN

Hmm. Yes.

　Silence.

CLAUDETTE

You want a sip?

　She hands him her cup of herbal tea. ANITA brings it over to him. He drinks some. ANITA stands nearby.

CLAUDETTE

You coming to bed?

MR. MANN

Not right away.

CLAUDETTE

Do you want me to stay up with you?

MR. MANN

No. I'm fine.

　ANITA takes the cup from him and gives it back to CLAUDETTE. The two women study him.

CLAUDETTE

Are you sure that's what's been making you sad? There isn't something else?

MR. MANN

No.

CLAUDETTE

There isn't someone else, is there?

MR. MANN
No.

> *CLAUDETTE crosses to him and gives him a kiss.*
> *ANITA leaves.*

CLAUDETTE
See you in a little while.

MR. MANN
(*nodding*) Hmm.

> *CLAUDETTE leaves.*
>
> *A moment goes by in silence.*
>
> *MR. MANN gets up. He's restless and so wanders around the room. He opens the window and hears the geese overhead. Suddenly, he goes to the door with the intention of leaving. A beat. He closes it gently.*
>
> *CHEBUTYKIN, a character from* Three Sisters, *appears. MR. MANN crosses, stands in front of him, and looks directly into his eyes.*

CHEBUTYKIN
"We don't live. We don't exist really. Nothing exists. We only believe we do."

> *CHEBUTYKIN disappears.*
>
> *We hear the geese flying over the house.*
>
> *MR. MANN shuts the window.*
>
> *Then he sits on the floor, under the window.*

THE DREAM

> *MR. MANN is seated. CLAUDETTE enters.*

MR. MANN
Claudette?

CLAUDETTE
Are you coming with me to take a look around? This is our new house. Do you like it?

MR. MANN

But it's just a corridor.

A woman dressed in the style of the early 1960s appears. She's all smiles.

MOTHER

My sweet darling boy!

MR. MANN

Mother!

She opens her arms to him. MR. MANN goes towards her but she walks right past him and greets and kisses her husband. Standing in a doorway, MR. MANN watches his parents kissing each other lovingly. He walks over to them. His mother turns to him and ... it's ANITA.

ANITA

An espresso, sir?

The FATHER takes MOTHER-ANITA in his arms and dances off with her. NICOLE walks through.

NICOLE

Outreach. Outreach. Get your copy here. *Outreach.*

MR. MANN follows NICOLE. She goes through one of the doors and shuts it behind her. He knocks on the door.

MR. MANN

Claudette! Claudette!

CLAUDETTE opens the door.

MR. MANN

Can I come in?

CLAUDETTE

You disappointed me. The other night.

MR. MANN

I'm sorry. I had too much to drink.

CLAUDETTE

If you want to go out with me, you're going to have to change.

She closes the door. He knocks again.

MR. MANN

Claudette! Let me in! Claudette!

MOMO opens the door instead of CLAUDETTE.

MOMO

Prends soin!

He leaves. MR. MANN follows him. He notices his FATHER lying on the ground.

MR. MANN

Dad!

FATHER

Help me, son.

MR. MANN

Dad! What have they done to you?

FATHER

I'm in a lot of trouble, my boy.

MR. MANN

You've got to help yourself, Dad! Don't let yourself go like this! You know what happens when you let yourself go. Dad!

MR. MANN tries to get his FATHER to stand but he sinks back down and then disappears.

MOMO passes with a flock of geese in his hands. MR. MANN follows him. Two doors open to reveal his two children. QUENTIN is writing on the palm of his hand. NADINE, as a child, sings a few lines of the lullaby "Hush, Little Baby." She comes over, gives him a kiss, and then runs off.

NADINE

Follow me, Dad!

He wants to follow her but QUENTIN stops him in order to show him what he's written on his palm.

QUENTIN

Look. It's your life.

MR. MANN

It's erasing itself very slowly.

QUENTIN

Yes.

> *QUENTIN leaves. There is less and less light. MR. MANN is caught between two doors.*

MR. MANN

Claudette! Where are you? I can't get out. Claudette!

> *Two nurses open the doors. SYLVAIN enters through the first door.*

MR. MANN

Sylvain! What are you doing here?

SYLVAIN

Hey! So that whole business about a corridor of light is true?

MR. MANN

Are you dead?

SYLVAIN

I've got a month left. I don't know that yet. I'm going to find out tomorrow morning. You'll never know either. I'm not going to tell anyone. The kids will make it through all right, but it's going to be much harder for Madeleine. What you'll say to her at the cemetery will be a great help. Thank you.

MR. MANN

Can I go with you, Sylvain?

SYLVAIN

Well sure, come on. It'll be fun. (*SYLVAIN goes through the second door.*) Hey! This place is fantastic. All my pain is gone.

MR. MANN

Really?

> *MR. MANN takes a few steps forward to follow SYLVAIN but stops at the threshold. We hear music.*

MR. MANN
   Hear that?

SYLVAIN
   What?

MR. MANN
   It's coming from Nadine's room. Wait.

SYLVAIN
   I can't. I can't stop.

MR. MANN
   I can't go, Sylvain! There's Nadine. I can't leave the children.

   SYLVAIN disappears. The doors close. MR. MANN wakes up.
   He is standing in front of Nadine's bedroom door. He's just
   woken up. He knocks gently on the door and then opens it.

NADINE

   MR. MANN stands at the doorway; NADINE sits at her desk.

NADINE
   Yes?

MR. MANN
   It's me. Can I come in?

NADINE
   Of course. What's the matter?

MR. MANN
   Nothing. I fell asleep on the couch. Your music woke me.

NADINE
   Sorry.

MR. MANN
   No, no. It doesn't matter. (*He listens.*) That's beautiful.

NADINE
   It's Bach.

   He listens. Beat.

NADINE

They're variations. Based on the same theme, he does a whole bunch of variations: forwards, backwards, in doubles, in canons.

MR. MANN

It's very beautiful.

Pause.

NADINE

Is something wrong?

MR. MANN

Oh ... no. It's just that ... I had this dream, I think ... I don't remember very much about it but ... it was very strange.

NADINE

You had a bad dream?

MR. MANN

Yes.

NADINE

Well ... come in.

MR. MANN

No, no, I don't want to disturb you.

NADINE

You're not disturbing me. Come in and sit down.

He enters. He sits down, deep in thought. She looks at him. He looks at his watch.

MR. MANN

One o'clock! Aren't you tired?

NADINE

No, it's my best time. Studying at night with music on, it's what I love most.

MR. MANN

What are you working on?

NADINE

Translation exercises.

"Ich spürte ihr gegenüber das wiedergeborene Lebenswünschen, wie jedes mal die Schönheit und das Glück uns Bewegt wurden."

MR. MANN

And in English?

NADINE

"I felt, standing there before her, the desire to live which is born again in us every time we come to the realization that we are face to face with beauty and happiness."

MR. MANN

That's good.

> *Pause.*

NADINE

If you don't mind, I'll keep working.

MR. MANN

Yes, yes, of course, I should let you ... (*stands to leave*)

NADINE

No. You can stay.

> *He sits back down. She goes back to her books. He watches her work. He is moved. He gets up.*

MR. MANN

Good night.

NADINE

Hey, Dad, wait!

> *She blows him a kiss, re-enacting one of their childhood rituals. He blows it back and then he leaves.*

> *MR. MANN enters his own bedroom. CLAUDETTE is sleeping. She is completely hidden by the blankets like someone who's dead. He uncovers her. She is naked. He looks at her as he takes off his shirt. Then he lays his face against her body.*

The next morning. MR. MANN is in the kitchen.

MR. MANN

Why did you have to wash all my shirts with your red one! I haven't got a single good shirt left! They're all ... pink now!

QUENTIN

Well, I had to do a wash and I saw your shirts there, so I said to myself ...

MR. MANN

Were you in that much of a hurry?

QUENTIN

Well ... yes. You could wear this one. I gave it to you and you've never worn it.

MR. MANN

It's a really nice shirt but I can't wear it to the office.

QUENTIN

Why not? It's one of a kind. Made by a local weaver. I think it'd be pretty cool if, in one of Quebec's leading institutions, you openly encouraged one of our own artisans.

MR. MANN

Of course. That's not –

QUENTIN

Would it go over better if you said an Inuit artist made it?

MR. MANN

Of course not! That's not the issue!

QUENTIN

I'd like it if you wore it once.

MR. MANN

All right ... okay. (*He puts it on.*) I'm not meeting with my boss this morning.

QUENTIN

That's too bad.

While his father is putting on the shirt, QUENTIN sits down.

QUENTIN

Yeah well, here's the thing ... I talked to Mom about this last night, and uh ... I'm leaving for Central America.

MR. MANN

Central America!

QUENTIN

Yeah. Six months. That's why I did the laundry last night.

MR. MANN

When?

QUENTIN

Well, like, right now.

MR. MANN

And you didn't think to mention it before this!

QUENTIN

Well ... I'm telling you now. I'm leaving with Latch and Ben. It's a thing, a project sponsored by CIDA. We're going to take Ben's Westfalia, drive down through the States, and after that head for Guatemala, I think. Then, Honduras. We're either going to dig wells or build schools. And when the contract's up, we might sign on for another stint or else we could decide to keep going farther south. You look surprised.

MR. MANN

Well ... yes ... a little! ... And, they're hiring you just like that. You guys have never built a thing in your entire lives!

QUENTIN

Well no, but ... for projects like this they don't necessarily need engineers or hydro-whatevers ... they just need people who ... who don't know how to do anything really. You don't think it's a good idea?

MR. MANN

No ... yes ... I do. I think ... (*pause*) Actually, I think it's a really great idea ...

QUENTIN

Yeah! It's 'cause they're really dealing with a lot of shit those people, you know. A whole lot of shit! And we – You know, even

geographically, we shit on them. I don't know if you can picture the
map of North America in your head, like ... okay, there's us, then the
States, and there at the bottom you've got Texas, Mexico, and after that
it gets narrower, kinda looks like a coccyx, and it's just like ... like we're
shittin' on them. All our shit ends up down there. It's as if all our crap –

MR. MANN

Yeah, yeah, it's okay, I get the picture.

QUENTIN

And the banks are eating them alive, you know. They're unbelievably in
debt. Coffee, well, it isn't worth anything anymore. So we feel the least
we can do is go give them a hand. Like, we all drink coffee, don't we!
Yeah, well ... what do you think?

MR. MANN

I think that ... yes. It's true! You're right! And if more people did
what you guys are doing, starting with our governments and the big
corporations, if everyone did a little bit more – Because, you know, if
there was just a little more respect and, when you get right down to it,
a little more love – that's the problem really. All the wars, the famines,
the exploitation, the pollution, when you get right down to it, it's
because of a ... a lack of love in the world!

>   *Beat.*

QUENTIN

Okay, I think I better get going.

MR. MANN

Right away?

QUENTIN

Well yeah, I've gotta get over to Latch's place. We're leaving tonight.

MR. MANN

All right then ... I want you to know that I'm really proud of you boys,
Quentin. I think it's a great idea, a great project. It's very generous of
you. It's ... it's noble.

QUENTIN

Thanks. Would you have a hundred dollars? For our first tank of
gas and ...

MR. MANN

Yes, sure. I don't know if I have that much on me.

QUENTIN

Give me what you've got.

MR. MANN

Here.

QUENTIN

Thanks.

MR. MANN

It's the right time for you to be travelling, Quentin. Go! After ... it'll be too late.

QUENTIN

Why?

MR. MANN

Well, after ... you'll be too busy, you won't be able to anymore.

QUENTIN

Come on, Dad, you can travel at any age. You could, too, if you wanted to.

MR. MANN

No. Not now. There're too many things ... You get locked in at a certain point in your life, you know. I should've done it before and ... what can I say ... I didn't!

QUENTIN

Why didn't you?

MR. MANN

Well ... why, why ... We got married young and then we had you and your sister right away.

QUENTIN

Did you have to get married?

MR. MANN

Course not. We wanted to get married. We wanted children ...

QUENTIN

Okay. And your job? Did you have to take it right away?

MR. MANN

No. But I was happy to get it. Back then, it was a job with a future.

QUENTIN

Okay. So, you've lived the life you wanted.

Pause.

MR. MANN

Well ... yes. I have.

QUENTIN

Okay. It's just that ... Look ...! I've gotta go. (*at the door*) Oh! I just wanted to say. You know, Mom's worried about you these days. She's a little sad, too, so ... I don't know ... get your ass in gear, Dad. I'm just saying this 'cause ... it'd be real nice if the two of you were still together when I get back, so ... do something. I'm just mentioning it, that's all.

MR. MANN

Yeah. Yes. Okay.

QUENTIN

Good. Well then ... see ya.

MR. MANN

See you. Hey! Cowboy!

This last line refers to a childhood game they used to play.
MR. MANN points two imaginary six-shooters at QUENTIN,
who draws his guns faster than his father and shoots.
MR. MANN pretends he's been hit. Laughter.
QUENTIN leaves.

MR. MANN

Good luck, son! Be careful! Say hi to Latch and Ben for me. Call us every now and then! Call us, okay? Goodbye, son!

MR. MANN watches his son leave.

CATHYA

It's the end of the workday. Office workers are heading home.

WOMAN 1

I was so happy! In the end, it wasn't Mark.

WOMAN 2

I know! It was his twin brother.

MAN 3

(*to MR. MANN*) Hey! Fantastic! That was a really good idea! We'll have to talk more about it. See you Monday.

MR. MANN

See you Monday.

> *MR. MANN goes to sit in the park. He takes off his jacket.*
> *He's wearing the shirt QUENTIN gave him. The shirt is one*
> *of a kind! It has a big, beautiful batik snowflake on the front.*
> *CATHYA, the young artist who was preparing an installation*
> *piece on snow in the first scene in the café, sits nearby.*
> *She notices his shirt.*

CATHYA

Excuse me, sir, it might seem strange for me to ask you this, but where did you get that shirt?

MR. MANN

Ah ... I don't know. It was a gift.

CATHYA

Okay. (*pause*) It's because I work in the visual arts –

MR. MANN

You're an artist?

CATHYA

Yes.

MR. MANN

My daughter's an artist too. She's a musician.

CATHYA

Oh really!

MR. MANN

Well now, she's studying languages, but she used to be a musician. She's an artist at heart.

CATHYA

Okay. Well, you see, I'm preparing an installation piece about snow.

MR. MANN

Snow?

CATHYA

Yes, on the uniqueness of the snowflake to be exact.

MR. MANN

Oh really!

CATHYA

Yes. And, ah ... well, to explain it to you simply, like ... there are scientists who have calculated that since there's been snow on Earth – these are very, very scientific calculations – they estimate that one million, billion, trillion snowflakes have fallen! And according to these scientists, there's a very good chance there's never been two alike.

MR. MANN

No!

CATHYA

Oh yes. And every snowflake is built essentially the same. They all have six branches. But, despite that limitation, Nature has somehow, well, how can I put it, it has like ... provided enough "free space" to allow for the creation of variations ad infinitum.

MR. MANN

They're all made the same but they're all diff–

CATHYA

Free.

MR. MANN

Oh I see ...

CATHYA

(*looking at his shirt*) And I'm sure there isn't another snowflake in the whole universe the same as that one right there.

MR. MANN

Oh no, I couldn't possibly give you this, it's ...

CATHYA

No, no!

MR. MANN

My son gave me this shirt and he just left on a humanitarian mission, so ...

CATHYA

Yes, sure, of course, I understand. Look, would you like to be a part of my vernissage? My opening?

MR. MANN

I've never been to a vernissage, I don't know how they work.

CATHYA

You wouldn't have to do anything.

MR. MANN

Nothing?

CATHYA

Not a thing. You'd just have to be ... like ... there and walk around with your snowflake.

MR. MANN

When would that be?

CATHYA

In four months. So you've got lots of time to think it over.

MR. MANN

Well ... why not? It could be fun.

CATHYA

Oh cool! Thank you. You'll have to give me your phone number.

MR. MANN

I'll give you my card. Here.

> MR. MANN hands CATHYA his card.

CATHYA

Thank you. Thank you so much. Oh my God! This is a sign! See you again soon.

MR. MANN
Goodbye.

He gets up, amused, and heads home.

ANITA

MR. MANN is at home. We hear music, the same music that was playing in the last scene in the café when he danced with ANITA. CLAUDETTE is getting ready to go out. She looks at herself in the mirror and adds a few final touches. She moves gently to the music. MR. MANN watches her.

CLAUDETTE
I like the CD you bought.

MR. MANN
Oh, I heard it on the radio the other day.

CLAUDETTE
It's really very good. Different. (*She looks at him.*) You make me laugh with that shirt.

MR. MANN
It was a big hit at the office.

CLAUDETTE
I'll be gone for an hour, an hour and a half. I'm coming straight home afterwards.

MR. MANN
Okay.

They look at each other. She leaves. He gets up and does a few little dance steps around the room. Suddenly, we hear the neighbour and her boyfriend shouting at each other.

ANITA
I'm fed up, do you hear me! It's always the same damn thing!

BOYFRIEND
I've had it! Go back to your mother's.

ANITA
I'm leaving. You'll never see me again.

BOYFRIEND

Fine! Here, take your things!

The sound of him throwing her suitcases at her.

ANITA

Hey! My suitcases!

BOYFRIEND

You're not leaving, I'm throwing you out!

The sound of the door as the boyfriend leaves. MR. MANN goes outside.

MR. MANN

Would you like me to call the ... (*He recognizes ANITA.*) Would you like me to call the police?

ANITA

No, no, it's okay.

MR. MANN

Do you need help?

ANITA

Could I call a cab from your house?

MR. MANN

Yes, of course, come in, come in.

ANITA

Thank you.

They enter his house.

ANITA

I'm sorry ... really ... I'm very, very sorry.

MR. MANN

No. It's all right. (*an awkwardness*) You live over there?

ANITA

Yes. I moved in with that loser six months ago! You ... you live here?

MR. MANN

Yes.

ANITA

Funny, eh, that we never ran into each other.

MR. MANN

Oh. There's such a turnover in your building we've stopped noticing.
And you and I don't keep the same hours.

ANITA

Of course we don't. (*She bursts into tears.*) I'm sorry!

MR. MANN

Did he hurt you?

ANITA

No, no. He just grabbed my arm. I gave him a good smack though.
Oh, I'm so fed up; I'm so, so fed up.

MR. MANN

Would you like to lie down for a little while?

ANITA

Thank you very much. This'll stop in a minute. (*She continues to cry.*)
Why do these things always happen to me? Why can't I have a normal
life like everybody else? This is what my life looks like! (*With her hand
in the air in front of her, she draws a broken line like a graph full of highs
and lows.*) It never lasts more than a year! I should know by now. Why
do all men turn into jerks after a while? It's always so much fun at the
beginning. If you only knew. He was so nice, so romantic, so intense.

MR. MANN

Yes, I know.

ANITA

...?

MR. MANN

When the windows are open, you know ... we could hear the intensity!
Quite well.

ANITA

Oh! You could hear us ...

MR. MANN

A little.

ANITA

Oh! I'm ... sorry.

MR. MANN

No, no.

ANITA

It's ... it's life, eh.

MR. MANN

Oh yes.

ANITA

My father used to always say: "Anita, one day, a man will come along who'll make you blossom. When that happens, you'll know he's the one." I thought I'd found him. Boy, was I wrong.

MR. MANN

Your father was a gardener?

ANITA

No, but he loved flowers. He used to say that everything in life ... has a secret calling as a flower. Nice, eh? And look! The poor man got a thistle for a daughter. (*She cries.*)

MR. MANN

You sure you wouldn't like a glass of water?

ANITA

No, no, thank you. I've got to go. I'm so very sorry. (*She looks at him.*) How do you do it? I watch you at the café. You always look so calm. Your life looks ... like this (*She draws a horizontal line in the air.*) How do you do it?

MR. MANN

Oh ... I ... I don't do anything. Nothing.

ANITA
   Nothing?

MR. MANN
   No, nothing.

ANITA
   (*looking at him as though he possesses one of the keys to the universe*)
   You're a wise man.

MR. MANN
   Oh ...

>   *We hear a knock on the door. MR. MANN goes to answer. It's
>   Anita's BOYFRIEND. He has a Kleenex stuffed up one of his
>   nostrils. He's had a nosebleed.*

BOYFRIEND
   Excuse me. Is Anita there?

MR. MANN
   Ah ...

>   *She signals to him that it's okay. The BOYFRIEND enters.*

ANITA
   What happened?

BOYFRIEND
   It's nothing. I'm sorry. It was my fault. Come with me, please? We'll talk
   things over. Calmly.

>   *Pause.*

ANITA
   Okay. I'm coming.

BOYFRIEND
   Do you want me to carry your suitcases?

ANITA
   That'd be nice of you.

>   *He picks them up.*

BOYFRIEND
   (*to MR. MANN*) I'm sorry.

MR. MANN
That's all right.

The BOYFRIEND leaves.

ANITA
I love him.

MR. MANN
Of course you do.

ANITA
Thank you for everything.

MR. MANN
It's nothing.

ANITA
Good thing you were there. I might've done something really stupid.

MR. MANN
Oh! Good Lord, don't ...

She moves closer to give him a kiss. He presents his cheek; she takes his mouth.

ANITA
I'll see you again soon.

MR. MANN
Yes. Soon.

She leaves. He's floating. He puts on his jacket, raises his arms in the air, and ... takes flight. As he flies through the sky, he crosses paths with the geese.

PRENDS SOIN

MOMO is walking along the street and waves to MR. MANN flying overhead. MR. MANN lands, then comes and sits next to him.

MOMO
You're not afraid.

MR. MANN
Sorry?

MOMO

    You're not afraid.

       MOMO gestures to indicate he could cut his throat.

MR. MANN

    You'd do something like that?

MOMO

    Course not. I'm as gentle as a lamb. *Prends soin.* Hey ... you're not supposed to be able to see me.

MR. MANN

    Oh no? How come?

MOMO

    (*showing him his cape*) The cape! It's a spy cape! I'm invisible.

MR. MANN

    Okay!

NICOLE

    (*entering*) Hey, my friend.

MOMO

    Nicole! Hi, Nicole!

       He gives her a big hug.

NICOLE

    Hey, Momo! You're my best friend, right?! Yessir, you're my bestest.

MOMO

    The best.

       We hear the geese overhead.

NICOLE

    Oh look! The geese!

MOMO

    The geese!

       MR. MANN, NICOLE, and MOMO watch the geese fly over. MOMO tries to imitate them.

MR. MANN

It must be fun to be able to fly like that.

MOMO

I can fly. My cape. It flies.

NICOLE

I wouldn't like it. Nope. Always the same. South in winter, north in summer. South in winter, north in summer.

MOMO

South winter, north summer, south, north ...

NICOLE

I couldn't go where I wanted to.

MOMO

Prends soin.

NICOLE

What does that mean, Momo? *Prends soin?* You say it all the time. *Prends soin. Prends soin. Prends soin.*

MOMO

Eh ...? I don't know.

MR. MANN

It means "take care."

NICOLE

What?

MR. MANN

Take care. Take care of others. Take care of yourself.

NICOLE

Wow! That's really radical!

MOMO

(*shooting his fist up in the air like a radical*) Yeah! *Prends soin!*

NICOLE

Hey, mister, you wanna buy the new issue?

MR. MANN

   Sure.

NICOLE

   Page eighteen, read it. I'm the one who wrote the poem.

MR. MANN

   Oh dear, I don't have any money on me. Here. Do you want my book
   in exchange?

NICOLE

   What is it?

MR. MANN

   A play.

NICOLE

   Like theatre? Wow! Momo's in plays, ya know.

MOMO

   Plays. At the Centre. In the activities like. It's hard. Have to learn the
   lines by heart, where to move, the emotions.

MR. MANN

   But are there things you enjoy?

MOMO

   Making love, costumes. And spies.

NICOLE

   (*examining the cover of the book*) *Three Sisters*.

MOMO

   I don't have any sisters. No brothers, no sisters. No hassles!

NICOLE

   (*She opens the book at random and she reads.*) Act ... eleven. Too-sen-
   back. "So you won't even allow us to dream of happiness?" Ver-shi-nin.
   (*She gets MOMO to read Vershinin's line.*) Look, Momo.

MOMO

   "No!"

NICOLE

Tuzenbach: "We don't understand each other, that's obvious. How can I convince you?" Che-boot ... Che-boot ... Too hard. "We're not alive."

MOMO

"We're not alive."

NICOLE

(*more softly*) "We don't exist."

MOMO

"We don't exist."

NICOLE

(*softly as if to herself*) "The world is a dream. We are the ones who created it."

MOMO

"The world is a dream. We are the ones who create it." .

Slowly his face changes and he becomes the actor who plays TUZENBACH. We hear TUZENBACH speaking as he walks onstage. The other actors arrive as well and take their respective places for the scene.

AT THE THEATRE

We're now in the theatre. MR. MANN is watching the play. NICOLE and MOMO have both become actors as well.

TUZENBACH

"Not merely in a couple of hundred years' time, but in a million years. Life doesn't change, it always goes on the same; it follows its own laws, which don't concern us, which we can't discover anyway. Think of the birds that migrate in the autumn, the geese for example. They fly on and on. It doesn't matter what thoughts they have in their heads, great ones or little ones, they fly on and on, not knowing where or why. And they'll go on flying no matter how many philosophers they happen to have flying with them. Let them philosophize as much as they like as long as they go on flying."

MR. MANN

    Excuse me, Baron Tuzenbach. This is closing night. I've come to see the play many times and that speech is my favourite. If it's not too much trouble, do you think you could say it again one last time for me, please?

TUZENBACH

    (*starting again slowly for MR. MANN*) "Not merely in a couple of hundred years' time ..."

    MR. MANN recites the beginning of the speech along with TUZENBACH, who will gradually stop speaking and let MR. MANN continue and finish in his own words.

TUZENBACH

    "... but in a million years. Life doesn't change, it always goes on the same; it follows its own laws ..."

MR. MANN

    "Life doesn't change, it goes on the same, with its own laws, laws which are beyond us, bigger than we are, and about which we know virtually nothing, but they still govern us and influence our lives. Take the birds that migrate, for example, the geese, the ducks, that fly over our heads every spring. They fly on and on, perhaps without even knowing why. It doesn't matter what sort of thoughts they might have in their heads, they fly on. And they go on flying even if there are philosophers flying with them, or poets or simpletons. Even if some of them are thinking grand thoughts and others are thinking nothing at all because they're too tired of flying. None of that matters, as long as they fly and keep on flying."

MASHA

    "All the same, isn't there some meaning to it all?"

MR. MANN

    Meaning? Look at the snow! What does it mean?!

    The actors stand and look at MR. MANN. They walk towards him as he walks through them. He turns and watches them enter the wings. Then, he walks off in the other direction entirely at his own pace.

END

PLAYWRIGHT'S ACKNOWLEDGEMENTS

I would like to thank the members of the acting company of
Lentement la beauté. They were there with me all through this
wonderful adventure, from the very first spark all the way to
the more than a hundred shows we performed. Thank you,
Marie-Josée, Lorraine, Hugues, Véronika, Pierre-François, and
Jack. For your talent and your generosity.

Thanks as well to Bertrand Alain, Christian Michaud, Caroline
Tanguay, and Réjean Vallée, who joined the team along the way.

An enormous thank-you to Peter Hinton and Paula Danckert
for being there at the start. They brought *And Slowly Beauty* to life
in English.

Thank you to Maureen Labonté for this beautiful translation
and for being such an attentive listener.

And thank you to Janet for the beauty, *la beauté qui bouleverse*.

– MICHEL NADEAU

TRANSLATOR'S ACKNOWLEDGEMENTS

It takes the commitment and resources of many individuals and organizations to bring a translation to fruition and then to the stage. My thanks go to:

- Peter Hinton, artistic director, and Paula Danckert, artistic associate and company dramaturg, English Theatre, the National Arts Centre in Ottawa. Paula's belief in Michel Nadeau's play led to the commissioning of this translation; Peter's to the premiere production of it as a co-production between the NAC and the Belfry Theatre in Victoria, British Columbia.

- Michael Shamata, artistic director of the Belfry and director of the premiere production. Your love of this play and your persistence helped make it all happen.

- Playwrights' Workshop Montreal for including the translation of *Lentement la beauté* in the 2009 Tadoussac Translation Residency. The work I was able to do there was invaluable. Special thanks go to Emma Tibaldo, artistic director, and June Park, managing director, for their enthusiasm and support of this project from the outset. And a very special thank-you to my dear friend and colleague, Linda Gaboriau, coordinator of the Tadoussac residency, for her insightful reading, helpful notes, and questions.

- Natasha Mytnowytch, Festival Coordinator, for the Canadian Stage Company Festival of Ideas and Creation for programming, in collaboration with the National Arts Centre's English Theatre program, *And Slowly Beauty*'s first reading in English.

- Thank you to the many wonderful actors who made invaluable contributions to this translation: Dennis Fitzgerald, Mary-Colin Chisholm, Caroline Gillis, Thomas Olajide, Christian Murray, Celine Stubel, Michael Simpson, Diane D'Aquila, Sarah Mennell, Kevin Bunday, Simon Rainville, and Natasha Greenblatt.

These acknowledgements would not be complete without extending my heartfelt thanks to publisher Kevin Williams and editors Ann-Marie Metten and Greg Gibson at Talonbooks. It was a true pleasure working with them on this book.

Finally, thank you to Michel Nadeau for writing such a beautiful play.

– MAUREEN LABONTÉ

Maureen Labonté is a dramaturg, translator, and teacher. She has also coordinated a number of play development programs in theatres and play development centres across Canada, including the Banff Centre for the Arts, the Centre des auteurs dramatiques (CEAD) in Montreal, the Shaw Festival, the National Arts Centre (Ottawa), and Playwrights' Workshop Montreal.

She was the jury chair for the Siminovitch Prize in Theatre from 2009 to 2012 and has taught at the National Theatre School of Canada since the mid-1990s. She worked at the Banff Playwrights Colony from 2003 to 2011, first as resident dramaturg, then as head of program, and finally as co-director.

Maureen Labonté has translated more than thirty-five Quebec plays into English. In addition to *And Slowly Beauty* by Quebec City director and playwright, Michel Nadeau, recent translations include *Porcupine (Porc-Epic)* by David Paquet for the Citadel Theatre in Edmonton. (*Porc-Epic* won the 2010 Governor General Award in Drama as well as the Michel Tremblay Prize. It was recently given a public reading at the Bushwacked Festival in Vancouver.) Her translation of Jean Marc Dalpé's *August, An Afternoon in the Country*, which premiered at Alberta Theatre Projects' playRites Festival, was produced this past fall at the Centaur Theatre in Montreal. It was published by Playwrights Canada Press in Spring 2013.

She lives in Montreal with her husband, playwright Jean Marc Dalpé, and their daughter, Marielle.

PHOTO: MICHAEL SLOBODIAN

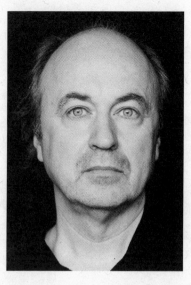

Michel Nadeau has been artistic director of Théâtre Niveau Parking since 1987. As a director, playwright, and actor, he has taken part in hundreds of theatre productions across Quebec. His directing credits include *La mort d'un commis voyageur*, *Le barbier de Séville*, *Jeanne et les anges*, and *Lentement la beauté (And Slowly Beauty)*. *Lentement la beauté* and *Jeanne et les anges*, both written and directed by Michel, were awarded the Masque de la production (Quebec theatre award) in 1995 and 2004.

In 2008, Michel directed *Regards-9*, co-produced with the Théâtre de la Bordée. *Regards-9* was part of the official events celebrating Quebec's 400th Anniversary.

In 2013, he directed *Félicité (Bliss)* by Olivier Choinière and *Cosmic Fear or the Day Brad Pitt Got Paranoia* by Christian Lollike.

Michel Nadeau conducts a parallel career as a teacher. A professor at the Conservatoire d'art dramatique de Québec since 1986, he teaches improvisation, movement, mask, *commedia dell'arte*, and all forms of clown. He served as director of the Conservatoire between 1996 and 2004 and, since 2007, he has headed the new "directing and creativity" section.

Very involved in the theatre community, Michel is a member of the boards of the Théâtre Périscope and the Conservatoire de musique et d'art dramatique du Québec, and he is vice-president of the Carrefour international de théâtre de Québec.

PHOTO: NICOLAS-FRANK VACHON